D0017014

English
Grammar
Handbook

Fredrik Liljeblad

Berlitz Publishing
New York   Munich   Singapore

English Grammar Handbook

No part of this book may be reproduced, stored in a retrieval system or transmitted in any form or means electronic, mechanical photocopying, recording or otherwise, without prior written permission from Apa Publications.

CONTACTING THE EDITORS
Every effort has been made to provide accurate information in this publication, but changes are inevitable. The publisher cannot be responsible for any resulting loss, inconvenience, or injury. We would appreciate it if readers would call our attention to any errors or outdated information by contacting Berlitz Publishing, 58 Borough High Street, London SE1 1XF, UK
Fax: (44) 20 7403 0290. email: comments@berlitzpublishing.com

All rights reserved.
© 2009 Apa Publications (UK) Ltd.

Berlitz Trademark Reg. U.S. Patent Office and other countries. Marca Registrada.
Used under license from Berlitz Investment Corporation.

Cover Photo © Punchstock / Stockbyte

Printed in China by CTPS, January 2012

Series Editor:

Christopher Wightwick is a former UK representative on the Council of Europe Modern Languages Project and principal inspector of Modern Languages for England.

CONTENTS

CONTENTS

A
THE BASICS

1

Talking About Things

a. Numbers, days, months, dates, and times

0 **zero** (usually pronounced "*oh*" in a series of numbers such as addresses or telephone numbers)

1	one	15	fifteen	28	twenty-eight
2	two	16	sixteen	29	twenty-nine
3	three	17	seventeen	30	thirty
4	four	18	eighteen	40	forty
5	five	19	nineteen	50	fifty
6	six	20	twenty	60	sixty
7	seven	21	twenty-one*	70	seventy
8	eight	22	twenty-two	80	eighty
9	nine	23	twenty-three	90	ninety
10	ten	24	twenty-four	100	one hundred
11	eleven	25	twenty-five		(OR a hundred)
12	twelve	26	twenty-six	1,000	one thousand
13	thirteen	27	twenty-seven		(OR a thousand)
14	fourteen				

Note: * In English, when you use letters to write the numbers from 21 to 29, 31 to 39, etc., up to 99, you always put a hyphen (-) between the two parts of the word.

twenty-five (25) **thirty-seven (37)** **fifty-one (51)**

Caution: Large numbers are often broken down into three-digit blocks that are separated by commas, not periods (1,000 or 5,000,000).

There are two different groups of numbers in English: cardinal and ordinal. The group that we've just covered (*1/one, 2/two, 3/three*) is called cardinal numbers. They are used for ordinary counting (*one, two, three; ten, twenty, thirty*). They are also used to talk about these concepts:

- **quantities of things**

  Ted has *seven* shirts.

  Maria speaks *three* languages.

  "A dozen" means *twelve* items.

  Please give me *five* bananas.

  We have *one* TV.

  Gone with the Wind has more than *one thousand* pages.

  My parents live in a *three*-room apartment.

- **time**

  There are *twenty-four* hours in a day.

  Lunch is at *twelve* o'clock.*

  I am only going to wait *fifteen* minutes.

  Jean's plane was *three* hours and *twenty-two* minutes late.

  Paul came to the United States *five* years ago.

  George Washington died about *two hundred* years ago.

Note: * See the end of this section for details about clock time.

- **age of people, animals, and things**

  John is *twenty-nine* (years old).

  I can't drink—I'm only *nineteen* (years old).

  My cat is *sixteen* (years old).

  This house is *seventy-five* years old.**

  Alexander the Great died at the age of *thirty-two*.

  The Coliseum in Rome is more than *two thousand* years old.

Note: ** With people and animals, adding "years old" is optional. With buildings or objects, you must add "years old" after the number.

THE BASICS

- **money**

That's $22.95 with tax.	(usually pronounced *twenty-two ninety-five*)
My plane ticket cost $250.00.	(*two hundred* and *fifty* dollars)
Todd paid less than $135,000 for his house.	(*one hundred/a hundred* and *thirty-five thousand* dollars)
Our car insurance is $98.50 a month.	(usually pronounced *ninety-eight fifty*)

- **arithmetic**

Two plus *two* is *four*.	$(2 + 2 = 4)$
Nine minus *eight* leaves *one*.	$(9 - 8 = 1)$
Four times *nine* is *thirty-six*.	$(4 \times 9 = 36)$
Sixty-three divided by *seven* is *nine*.	$(63 \div 7 = 9)$

Does *thirty-three* plus *two hundred seventy-four* (33 + 274) equal *three hundred* and *seven* or *three hundred* and *nine* (307/309)?

- **numbers in a series (page or chapter numbers in books; passport, driver's license, and credit card numbers; hotel room numbers or addresses; telephone numbers)**

In writing, numbers used in this way are almost always written with numerals, not spelled out.

My license number is B5429816.	(*five-four-two-nine-eight-one-six*)
That's American Express, 6573 594842 23771.	(*six-five-seven-three, five-nine-four-eight-four-two, two-three-seven-seven-one*)
Tony's address is 35088 Thomas Boulevard.	(*three-five-oh-eight-eight*)
Teresita's restaurant is at 4405 Berkeley.	(*four-four-oh-five* OR *forty-four oh-five*—both pronunciations can be used with four-digit address numbers)
I'm at the Savoy, room 2112.	(*two-one-one-two* OR *twenty-one twelve*—both pronunciations can be used with four-digit room numbers)

Phone numbers are always pronounced with a pause between the first three digits and the last four digits. You may hear some people pronounce the last four digits in groups of two (887-2755/"*eight-eight-seven, twenty-seven, fifty-five*"), but most people don't.

Our phone number is (212) 675-7122.	(two-one-two, six-seven-five, seven-one-two-two)

The other group of numbers is called ordinal numbers (first, second, third, etc.).

(the) 1st	(the) first	(the) 20th	(the) twentieth
(the) 2nd	(the) second	(the) 21st	(the) twenty-first*
(the) 3rd	(the) third	(the) 22nd	(the) twenty-second
(the) 4th	(the) fourth	(the) 23rd	(the) twenty-third
(the) 5th	(the) fifth	(the) 24th	(the) twenty-fourth
(the) 6th	(the) sixth	(the) 25th	(the) twenty-fifth
(the) 7th	(the) seventh	(the) 26th	(the) twenty-sixth
(the) 8th	(the) eighth	(the) 27th	(the) twenty-seventh
(the) 9th	(the) ninth	(the) 28th	(the) twenty-eighth
(the) 10th	(the) tenth	(the) 29th	(the) twenty-ninth
(the) 11th	(the) eleventh	(the) 30th	(the) thirtieth
(the) 12th	(the) twelfth	(the) 40th	(the) fortieth
(the) 13th	(the) thirteenth	(the) 50th	(the) fiftieth
(the) 14th	(the) fourteenth	(the) 60th	(the) sixtieth
(the) 15th	(the) fifteenth	(the) 70th	(the) seventieth
(the) 16th	(the) sixteenth	(the) 80th	(the) eightieth
(the) 17th	(the) seventeenth	(the) 90th	(the) ninetieth
(the) 18th	(the) eighteenth	(the) 100th	(the) (one) hundredth
(the) 19th	(the) nineteenth	(the) 1000th	(the) (one) thousandth

THE BASICS

Note: * When you use letters to write the ordinal numbers from 21 to 29, 31 to 39, etc., up to 99, you always put a hyphen (-) between the two parts of the word. Ordinal numbers are usually used with *the* in front of them. When we write them with numerals, we often (but not always) write the last two letters of the word smaller than usual and slightly above the last digit.

(the) **twenty-fifth** (the 25th or 25th)
(the) **thirty-seventh** (the 37th or 37th)
(the) **fifty-first** (the 51st or 51st)

English uses ordinal numbers to show the order of several things, people, or events—which comes first, second, or last.

This is Ellen's *third* job in a year.
Ted was our *first* child.
The Johnsons bought a *second* car last week.

We also use ordinal numbers to talk about these concepts:

• specific dates or months

Harry's wedding is January *28th.*
The Fourth of July is a big holiday.
Christmas is always on December *25th.*
November is *the eleventh* month of the year.
Let's meet again on *the 10th* of this month.

• floors or stories in a building

Joe works on *the 25th* floor of this building.
This elevator only goes from *the 21st* floor to the *50th* floor.
The workers are finishing the building's *fifth* story.

- the order of steps in a procedure, or of events in a story

> *First*, wash the vegetables.
> *First*, Bill isn't doing a good job; *second*, he has a bad attitude; *third*, the boss doesn't like him.

- grading similar things in a group according to a specific set of rules, categories, or for quality *(Cardinal numbers are seldom used for this concept.)*

> The color of this diamond is only *fifth*-rate.
> Leo's son was *second* in his class at law school.
> Which team came in *fourth*?
> Tom was *first* across the finish line at the race.
> Burton's dog took only *fifth* place at the dog show.

- listing things, events, or people in a definite order

> My *first* mistake was asking for my *third* drink.
> That new diet book moved from *10th* to *6th* place on the bestseller list.
> Welcome to the *69th* annual Academy Awards show.

One of the few times English combines cardinal and ordinal numbers is when we talk about certain fractions (2/5 = *two-fifths*; 1/7 = *one-seventh*; 3/8 = *three-eighths*, etc.). The first part of such a fraction is a cardinal number, the second half is an ordinal number. Common fractions are irregular: 1/2 (*one-half/a half*), 1/4 (*one-quarter /one-fourth*), and 3/4 (*three-quarters/three-fourths*).

> *Four-fifths* of the class were not late once this year. My school report is *two-thirds* done.

THE BASICS

The days of the week:

Sunday	Wednesday	Friday
Monday	Thursday	Saturday
Tuesday		

The days from Monday to Friday are called *weekdays*. Saturday and Sunday are called *the weekend*.

These are the months of the year:

January	April	July	October
February	May	August	November
March	June	September	December

In English, days of the week and months of the year are always written with a capital (big) letter.

There are two ways to refer to dates:

March 17th	OR	(the) 17th (of) March

The first way is more common in the United States; the second is more common in Britain. In the United States, when you see the date and month in numerals (10/5, 4/9, 12/3), the number for the month always comes first (10/5 always means October 5th, *not* May 10th). In Britain, it is the opposite: 10/5 is May 10th.

There are two ways of writing clock times in English:

1:00	one o'clock	5:00	five o'clock
2:00	two o'clock	6:00	six o'clock
3:00	three o'clock	7:00	seven o'clock
4:00	four o'clock	8:00	eight o'clock

8

9:00	nine o'clock	11:00	eleven o'clock
10:00	ten o'clock	12:00	twelve o'clock (noon or midnight)

There are also two ways of saying these times. Most people usually say the numerals (5:00) as "five" without saying "o'clock."

See you at 7:00. (*seven*)
Arrive at the airport before 2:00. (*two*)

This is the way to give clock times other than the exact hour:

5:00	five o'clock	
5:05	five-oh-five	OR five (minutes) past five
5:07	five-oh-seven	
5:10	five-ten	OR ten (minutes) past five
5:12	five-twelve	
5:15	five-fifteen	OR a quarter past five
5:22	five twenty-two	
5:30	five-thirty	OR half past five
5:35	five thirty-five	
5:45	five forty-five	OR a quarter to six
5:49	five forty-nine	
5:57	five fifty-seven	

Here are some other things to remember about clock time.

- People may sometimes add "o'clock" to emphasize the exact hour, but never with any other clock time. For a time like 2:30, you can say *two-thirty*, or you can say *half past two* (they are interchangeable), but you cannot say *two-thirty o'clock.*

- If you mean twelve o'clock (12:00) at night, you say *midnight* (or sometimes *twelve midnight*). For twelve o'clock (12:00) during the day, you say *noon* (or sometimes *twelve noon*).

THE BASICS

- In the United States, only the military uses the twenty-four-hour clock. For times between midnight and noon, add *a.m.* after the time. If the time is between noon and midnight, add *p.m.*, but only if the listener could misunderstand. Usually, the rest of the sentence clearly explains which time we mean. Sometimes, we also add *a.m.* or *p.m.* for emphasis.

Mr. Smith is taking the 10:00 p.m. flight to Rome. (avoids confusion with the 10:00 a.m. flight)

Does your father know it's 5:00 a.m. here? (for emphasis)

We'll be at the station between 11:00 a.m. and noon.

- The use of *a.m.* and *p.m.* are for the exact hour. People almost never say *6:37 p.m.* Instead, they usually add *in the morning, in the afternoon, in the evening,* or *at night.* In most cases, this is not necessary.

"What time does the plane arrive?" →→→ **"It arrives at 7:45."**

"Is that 7:45 in the morning?" →→→ **"No. That's 7:45 in the evening."**

- Never add *o'clock* to *a.m.* or *p.m.*

- When telling someone the time, English uses the phrase *it's*—a short form (*contraction*) of *it is*. (See Chapter 2, section f; *Contractions with verbs,* and also this chapter, section e, *It.*)

"Do you have the time?" →→→ **"*It's* exactly one o'clock."**

"What time is it, please?" →→→ **"*It's* four-twenty-two."**

"Could you give me the time?" →→→ **"*It's* about two."**

b. Articles—a and the

In an English sentence, the word for a person, animal, thing, or idea is called a *noun*. The words *boy, cat, pen,* and *love* are all nouns.

When we talk about a noun, we usually use one of two words in front of it: *a* (*an* in front of a word that starts with the sound of *a, e, i, o, u*) or *the*. These words are called *articles*.

English uses *a/an* (also called indefinite articles):

- to talk about a noun in a general sense (more details may come later)

This is *a* small gift for you.
I want *a* dog.
Do you have *a* map?
There is *a* phone call for Rob Carlson.
Please give me *an* ice cream cone.
May I have *a* glass of water?
Is there *a* gas station near here?

- to talk about one noun out of a specific group

I'm looking for *a* book about gardening.
Father is *an* artist.
Is there *a* boy named Peter here?
I'd like *a* steak with fried potatoes.
An orange has a lot of vitamin C.
Did *a* cat run past you just now?
We saw *a* famous play by Shakespeare.

- to give a list of nonspecific, general things

He had *an* overcoat, *a* pair of brown shoes, and *an* old hat.
You will need *a* paintbrush, *a* sponge, and *a* pail of water.

11

THE BASICS

English uses *the* (also called a definite article):

- to talk about one specific noun (or a specific group of nouns)

This is *the* only painting by Leonardo in a private collection.
The Kohinoor is *the* largest diamond in the world.
Who is driving *the* car? (our car)

- to talk about one specific noun in a general group

Peter is *the* boy with red hair.	(no other boy in the group has red hair)
The Malone family lives in *the* gray house.	(only one gray house on the street)
Who is *the* woman with the dog?	(several women; only one has a dog)
I'd like *the* fish next to the basket of shrimp.	(many fish; one is next to the shrimp)

- to talk about a specific noun that the speaker and listener recognize

How would you like *the* steak, sir? Medium?	(the steak the man asked for)
Do you want *the* paperback edition or *the* hardcover edition?	(they both know the name of the book)
***The* room has a view of *the* park.**	(they both know which room; there is only one park near the building)

Sometimes we don't use any article at all. If you talk about a subject in a general way, or if you say something most people agree with, you seldom use any article. In these examples, most of the nouns are in plural form (see section c, *Nouns— one or more*).

12

Big *cars* use a lot of gas. (BUT *The* big *car* over there uses a lot of gas.)

Children have so much energy. (BUT *A child* of seven always has so much energy.)

I think *music* is very relaxing. (BUT I think *the music* in this restaurant is very relaxing.)

Cats are very independent. (BUT *A cat* is more independent than *a dog*.)

Doctors have no private lives. (BUT *The doctors* in this hospital have no private lives.)

Here are some other things to remember about articles:

- If a word is not used for its true meaning as part of a sentence, we don't use any article.

What does the word *factory* mean? (BUT *The* factory in our town is moving.)

What time does *Flight to Wonderland* start? (name of movie) (BUT What time does *the flight* to Paris leave?)

- If *the* comes in front of a word that starts with the sound of *a, e, i, o, u,* it is pronounced *thee.*

the (*thee*) Edo river
the (*thee*) Edwardian era
the (*thee*) end of the week
the (*thee*) edge

English does not put *the* in front of people's names, or the actual names of countries or most cities, but when we talk about someone only by his or her title, we usually use *the* (or, in a few cases, *a*).

THE BASICS

The President of the United States	(BUT **former President Jimmy Carter**)
The Queen of England	(BUT **Queen Elizabeth**)
The Pope	(BUT **Pope John Paul**)
Madonna	(BUT *the* **rock star, Madonna**)

c. Nouns—one or more

A noun is the word (or words) in a sentence that describes a person, animal, thing, or idea. An English noun has two general forms, the *singular* form (when the word stands for one person, animal, thing, etc.) and the *plural* form (when the word stands for two or more).

About ninety percent of all English nouns usually just add -s to the singular to form the plural.

singular		plural
one boy	→→→	two boys
the pretty girl	→→→	the pretty girls
a dog	→→→	five dogs
a house	→→→	many houses

Sometimes the spelling of the word changes slightly from singular to plural. There are some spelling rules that show how these words change. These changes don't have many exceptions.

singular form ends in		plural form adds
• -ch	→→→	-es
ben*ch*	→→→	bench*es*
chur*ch*	→→→	church*es*
sear*ch*	→→→	search*es*

• -s/-ss	→→→	-es
ga*s*	→→→	gas*es*
cla*ss*	→→→	class*es*
ma*ss*	→→→	mass*es*
• -sh	→→→	-es
cra*sh*	→→→	crash*es*
eyela*sh*	→→→	eyelash*es*
• -x	→→→	-es
bo*x*	→→→	box*es*
se*x*	→→→	sex*es*
• -y	→→→	-ies*
countr*y*	→→→	countr*ies*
fl*y*	→→→	fl*ies*
lad*y*	→→→	lad*ies*

Note: * If the *y* follows a vowel (*boy, play*, etc.), the plural is *-s*, not *-ies* (*boys, plays*, etc.).

The spelling rules of the plural forms shown next are more irregular. These changes have some exceptions, so check a dictionary to be sure.

singular form ends in		**plural form usually adds**
• -f/-fe	→→→	-ves
hal*f*	→→→	hal*ves*
shel*f*	→→→	shel*ves*
wi*fe*	→→→	wi*ves*
BUT		
roo*f*	→→→	roof*s*

THE BASICS

• -o	→→→	-es
buffalo	→→→	buffalo(e)s (e optional)
cargo	→→→	cargo(e)s (e optional)
hero	→→→	heroes
potato	→→→	potatoes
tomato	→→→	tomatoes

These changes are completely irregular. Just memorize them.

singular form		plural form
foot	→→→	feet
man	→→→	men
mouse	→→→	mice
person	→→→	people
tooth	→→→	teeth
woman	→→→	women

singular form		plural form adds -en/-ren
child	→→→	children
ox	→→→	oxen

Some words have exactly the same plural as the singular form. Here are a few of them.

(1) deer	→→→	(20) deer
(1) fish	→→→	(8) fish*
(a) series	→→→	(many) series
(1) sheep	→→→	(3) sheep

Note: * The plural *fishes* means "many different kinds of fish."

These number words usually have the same plural form as the singular.

(a/1) dozen	→→→	**(5) dozen** (1 dozen = 12 pieces)
(a/1) hundred	→→→	**(7) hundred**
(a/1) thousand	→→→	**(30) thousand**

When we use these words generally (without an exact number in front of them), we are really saying "very, very many." Then we add -s to the plural form, usually followed by *of*.

I have two dozen friends. (BUT I have dozens *of* friends.)

Jessica has over 500 shoes! (BUT Jessica has hundreds *of* shoes!)

Martin needs ten thousand dollars. (BUT Martin needs thousands *of* dollars.)

Some words have no singular form; we always use them in a plural sense.

clothes	**mankind** (human beings)
(eye)glasses	**pants/trousers**
jewelry	**scissors**

If we want to show that we mean only one, we usually use certain words followed by *of*.

an item of clothing	*a piece of* jewelry
a pair of (eye)glasses	*a (pair of)* scissors

17

THE BASICS

We use some nouns to talk about ideas or feelings. Usually, these *concept nouns* don't have a plural.

calculation (planning, *not* mathematics)
courage
fear
hate
knowledge
love
patience
understanding

We sometimes add an *-s* to show that this feeling happened many times or that there are several kinds of, for instance, love.

Paul's *ambition* can be a problem sometimes. (BUT Paul has many *ambitions*.)
***Love* is powerful. (BUT He has only two *loves:* money and cars.)**

Some words from foreign languages (especially Greek, Latin, and French) have "unusual" plural forms. Here are a few, but there are others. Many foreign words in English just have an *-s* in the plural form (*typhoons; kindergartens; tortes*), so check a dictionary to be sure.

alumn**us**	→→→	alumn**i**
analys**is**	→→→	analys**es**
appendi**x**	→→→	appendi**ces**
beau	→→→	beau**x** (boyfriend/s)
cact**us**	→→→	cact**i**
cris**is**	→→→	cris**es**
criteri**on**	→→→	criteri**a**
cul-de-sac	→→→	cul**s**-de-sac
medi**um**	→→→	medi**a**
memorand**um**	→→→	memorand**a**
parenthes**is**	→→→	parenthes**es**
phenomen**on**	→→→	phenomen**a**

d. Noun substitutes—possessives and pronouns

When we speak generally about a person or thing (man, dog, river), we call it a *common noun.* If we speak about a specific person or thing (Bob, Lassie, the Mississippi River), it becomes a *proper noun.* We write the first letter of proper nouns with capitals; we use only small letters to write common nouns.

When we want to show that one noun "belongs to" or is connected with another noun, we use a *possessive.* It shows the relationship between two or more people or things. The most common possessive in English is *'s.* The position of the *apostrophe* (') is important.

the book's cover	(one "owner," one item)
the book's covers	(one "owner," two items)
the boys' book	(two "owners," one item)
the boys' books	(two "owners," two items)

As mentioned earlier (see section c, *Nouns—one or more*), a few plurals in English are irregular. One noun already means two or more people or things. With these nouns, we form the possessive like this:

the people's choice
the women's clothes
the children's laughter

There are two other possessive forms that we often use as substitutes for the *noun + 's*. We use these possessives often, especially with proper nouns, to avoid repeating the *noun + 's* many times.

Bob drives *Bob's* car to *Bob's* office.	→→→	**Bob drives *his* car to *his* office.**
	OR	
This car is *Bob's.*	→→→	**This car is *his.***

If the possessive comes *before* the noun, it takes the form in the first example (called a *possessive adjective*). If it comes *after* the noun, it takes the slightly different form of the second example (called a *possessive pronoun*).

Possessive adjectives (*before* noun)

my (car, etc.)	= the speaker's
your	= one or more listener's
his	= a male person's or animal's
her	= a female person's or animal's
its	= a "thing's" or unnamed animal's
our	= the speaker's and listener's (or the speaker's and a third person's)
their	= two or more persons, animals, or things (*not* the speaker's or the listener's)

Jean is *my* second wife.

Is *your* house a three- or four-bedroom model?

I don't know *his* name.

What is *her* address?

Mrs. Simpson's old Rolls Royce still has *its* original paint.

Today is *our* 15th wedding anniversary.

Beth and Joe lost all *their* money in bad investments.

Possessive pronouns (replace the noun)

mine	= the speaker's
yours	= one or more listener's
his	= a male person's or animal's
hers	= a female person's or animal's
____	(no form for "it")
ours	= the speaker's and listener's (or the speaker's and a third person's)
theirs	= two or more persons, animals, or things (not the speaker's or the listener's)

The gray coat is *mine*. (*my coat*)

Is this dog *yours*? (*your dog*)

This glass isn't mine, it's *his*. (*his glass*)

The two blond girls are *hers*. (*they are her daughters*)

The Rossignol skis are *ours*, not *theirs*. (*our skis*)

The house with the red roof is *theirs*. (*their house*)

When we want to speak about one or more proper or common nouns in detail, but not in terms of possession, we can avoid repeating the same noun by using a substitute for that noun—a *pronoun*.

Bob and Mary live in a house. Bob and Mary have three children. Bob and Mary both like music. Bob likes jazz, but Bob does not like country music. Mary does not like jazz, but Mary likes country music.

THE BASICS

Without pronouns, we must repeat *Bob, Mary,* or *Bob and Mary* many times. If we use pronouns, we can avoid that and also make the sentences smoother to say and easier to listen to. Now read the same paragraph about Bob and Mary, but this time with pronouns replacing most of the proper nouns.

> **Bob and Mary live in a house. <u>They</u> have three children. <u>They</u> both like music. Bob likes jazz, but <u>he</u> does not like country music. Mary does not like jazz, but <u>she</u> likes country music.**

Each of the underlined words is a pronoun. *He* replaces *Bob,* *she* replaces *Mary,* and *they* replaces *Bob and Mary.* There are many kinds of pronouns in English, and each pronoun has a particular purpose. Pronouns that replace the noun (or nouns) for the person or thing are called *personal pronouns.* Just like possessives, personal pronouns have two forms, the *subject form* and the *object form.* Let's look at the subject form first.

Personal pronouns (subject form)

I	= the speaker
you	= one or more listeners
he	= a male person or animal
she	= a female person or animal
it	= a "thing" or unnamed animal*
we	= the speaker and listener (or the speaker and a third person)
they	= two or more persons, animals, or things (not the speaker or listener)

Note: * See section e, *It,* for other meanings of *it.*

In almost all English sentences, one person (or thing) *does* something. One word shows us what that action is (the *verb*), and the noun shows us who or what is doing the action. That noun is called the *subject* of the sentence. The pronoun can also be the subject when we substitute a subject-form pronoun for a common or proper noun.

22

<u>Bill</u> jogs every morning. →→→ <u>He</u> jogs every morning.

<u>Janet</u> drives to work. →→→ <u>She</u> drives to work.

<u>The roses</u> are blooming. →→→ <u>They</u> are blooming.

These personal pronouns are used to replace the proper and common nouns that are the subjects of the sentences.

Often, one noun "does" something to another noun. The first noun (the one that does the action) is the subject. In English sentences, the verb always follows the subject. The second noun often receives the action (or the effect of the action). That second noun is the object. The object always follows the verb. In the sentences that follow, the subject(s) or pronoun(s) is underlined once, and the object is underlined twice.

<u>Tom and I</u> drink <u>tea</u>. →→→ <u>We</u> drink <u>tea</u>.

<u>Sara</u> has <u>a book</u>. →→→ <u>She</u> has <u>a book</u>.

<u>Mike</u> dislikes <u>cats</u>. →→→ <u>He</u> dislikes <u>cats</u>.

<u>Joann</u> has <u>your keys</u>. →→→ <u>She</u> has <u>your keys</u>.

We will learn more about objects later (see Chapter 3, section a, *The basic English sentence*), but they are important here because the other form of personal pronouns replaces objects, not subjects.

Personal pronouns (object form)

me	= the speaker
you	= one or more listeners
him	= a male person or animal
her	= a female person or animal
it	= a "thing" (or unnamed animal)
us	= the speaker and listener (or the speaker and a third person)
them	= two or more persons, animals, or things (not the speaker or listener)

THE BASICS

Look at these sentences again, this time with pronouns replacing both the subjects *and* objects.

Tom and I drink <u>tea</u>. →→→ <u>We</u> drink <u>it</u>.
Sara has <u>a book</u>. →→→ <u>She</u> has <u>it</u>.
<u>Mike</u> dislikes <u>cats</u>. →→→ <u>He</u> dislikes <u>them</u>.
<u>Joann</u> has <u>your keys</u>. →→→ <u>She</u> has <u>them</u>.

Of course, you can't substitute pronouns for any noun until both the speaker and listener understand exactly which noun the pronoun is replacing. In the following sentences, the subject pronouns are underlined once, the object pronouns twice.

<u>You</u> are looking for Bob? <u>I</u> see <u>him</u> over there.
<u>She</u> wrote to <u>us</u> twice.
Why did <u>they</u> call <u>us</u>? <u>I</u> don't want to talk to <u>them</u>.
<u>She</u> left her bag outside and the rain ruined <u>it</u>.
They spoke with Joe, but <u>they</u> didn't fire <u>him</u>.
You always take the kids to school—<u>I</u>'ll drive <u>them</u> today.
I don't like that jacket. Why did <u>you</u> buy <u>it</u>?

e. It

We learned in section d that *it* means a thing or animal, but English also uses *it* in a second way. When we say "*it's* three o'clock," or "*it's* raining," what do we mean by *it*?

English sometimes uses *it* in this way to mean things like "this action" or "this situation." Often, when we say "it's cold," we can't clearly understand what *it* really means—the temperature or the way the speaker feels? This form of *it* almost always starts the sentence. Here are some of the ways we use this form of *it*.

- to talk about weather or temperature

It's snowing.   (It's = It is)
It's hot today.
It's starting to rain.
It's hurricane season now.

- to talk about clock time or length of time

It's ten o'clock.
It's almost Christmas.
It's two days since the fire.
It usually takes an hour to get to the office.

- to talk about nature or something we can't control

It gets dark by 5:00 in December.
It will soon be spring.
It's too late to catch the plane.
It's hard (for me) to understand algebra.
It's expensive to have three children in college.
It's easy to drive a truck.
It hurts. (this part of my body hurts)

f. Prepositions—connecting two nouns

When we talk about the physical position of two or more nouns (the sofa and table in a living room, a book and a magazine, our neighbor's house and our own house), we need one or more small words—*prepositions*—to show where they are.

25

THE BASICS

English has many prepositions. Some of the most important are:

above/below
at
behind/in front of
between
in
near
next to
on/under

The school is *next to* the library.

The supermarket is *in front of* Bill's house.

Bill's house is *behind* the supermarket.

The bus station is *near* Ellen's house.

The movie theater is *between* the café and the bookshop.

Tom and Jackie's apartment is *above* the restaurant.

Tom and Jackie's apartment is *under* Helen's apartment.

The flower shop is *in* the mall, *on* the first floor.

The doctor's office is *at* the corner of 5th and Market Streets.

It's important to remember that you usually can't change the order of the nouns and keep the correct meaning. If the movie theater is between the café and the bookshop, then it is also between the bookshop and the café. But if Tom and Jackie's apartment is under Helen's apartment, then Helen's apartment can't be under Tom and Jackie's apartment.

There are other prepositions in English, and we will study them later in the book.

2 Talking About Actions and Being

a. Verbs—all about time

We use verbs to show what is happening to the person, animal, or thing we are talking about—the *subject* (see Chapter 3, section a; *The basic English sentence*). In dictionaries, verbs are listed in their infinitive form. We need verbs to explain any action, thought, feeling, or change (or even to explain that there is no change) in a situation. Verbs give us this information in three important ways:

- They tell us that the subject does or does not do something.

I *play* golf.
Michael *plays* tennis.
We *play* baseball.

- They give information on the person the sentence is about.

I *am* American.
Raoul *is* French.
You *are* a friend.
Paul and Margaret *are* my neighbors.
Robert *lives* in a house.
Robert *does not live* in an apartment.
We *have* two children.
We *do not have* five children.

• They show when the action is happening.

I *live* in New York.
Sara *lived* in New York in 1993.
Gena and Roger *are living* in London now.
My sister *will be living* in New York next year.
Larry *has lived* in New York since 1979.

In English, *when* something happens is very important. Verbs change in spelling or pronunciation to show when the action is happening—in the past, future, or present (talk*ed*—*will* talk—*am/is/are* talk*ing*). These changes are called *tenses*, and each tense is used in a special way. Tenses are mostly about the time of an action, but each tense also tells us if the action is regular or special, if two actions are happening at the same time, if an action was interrupted by something else, etc.

While I *was eating*, the phone rang. (interruption)
While I *was eating* dinner, my son *was watching* TV.
(something happening at the same time)

Most English verbs form tenses in the same ways, such as adding -*ed* to a verb to show a past action. Verbs that do this are called *regular verbs*. Some verbs form these tenses in other ways. These are called *irregular* verbs.

b. Types of verbs—describing actions, situations, or feelings

Most verbs describe a physical movement or change—actions. This gives verbs their importance. Verbs tell us about things that are happening.

The car sped forward.
The rain *poured* down out of the sky.
Music *blared* from the stereo.
The thirsty man *gulped* the water.

TALKING ABOUT ACTIONS AND BEING

These action verbs, especially in a *progressive* tense (see section e; *Simple and progressive verb forms*), can tell the listener many things about a situation. They can show:

- a gradual change from one period of a person's life to another

to accelerate

to age

to become

to broaden

to change

to decrease

to grow

to increase

to slow

to speed

His parents *were growing* older.

Prices *have become* unreasonable.

The girls' childhoods *are* really *speeding* by.

- daily actions or an action of the moment

to ask

to drink

to drive

to eat

to listen

to read

to run

to talk

to throw

to watch

to work

to write

I *threw* the ball while my parents *were watching*.
The professor always *asks* many questions in the lecture.
My father *worked* in a steel mill every day of his life.

- a change from one place to another

to discover
to explore
to investigate
to journey
to move
to search
to seek
to travel
to uncover
The police *searched* the forest from one end to the other.
Many people *have explored* the Amazon River.
Howard Carter *discovered* the treasure of Tutankhamun.

- the things that happen in illnesses (or other physical reactions)

to ache
to burn (with fever)
to cough
to groan
to itch
to moan
to scratch
to sneeze
to sweat
My head *ached* and I *coughed* all night.
Helen's eyes always *itch* in spring.
The fever made Michael *sweat*.

TALKING ABOUT ACTIONS AND BEING

Although action verbs show things happening and changing, many other verbs show feelings or situations with little change.

I *remember* my mother *loved* the month of June.

The flowers in her garden *smelled* wonderful.

The sunshine *felt* good.

There are several groups of these nonaction verbs, usually called *state-of-being* verbs. These state-of-being verbs usually show thinking, feeling, one of the five senses, or the relation between two things or people. The most common state-of-being verb is *be*. Here are some more:

- These verbs show the way one of the five senses identifies something.

to appear

to feel

to hear

to look (like)

to seem

to smell

to sound

to taste

- These verbs show some form of thinking or feeling.

to believe	to hate	to prefer	to understand
to doubt	to know	to remember	to want
to fear	to like	to think (of)	to wish
to forget	to love		

THE BASICS

- These verbs show the relationship between things or people.

to belong (to)
to contain
to have
to lack
to matter
to mean
to owe
to own

- These verbs can show either a state of being or an action, depending on how you use them in a sentence.

to ache
to be
to cost
to equal
to hurt
to itch
to measure
to weigh

Sometimes the action and state-of-being forms of the verb are exactly the same; sometimes they are quite different.

I can *feel* the softness of this wool blanket.	(action)
The blanket *feels* good (to me).	(state of being)
The children *are looking* at the dessert.	(action)
This food *looks* delicious.	(state of being)

I *smell* smoke from the barbecue.	(action)
That soup *smells* spicy.	(state of being)
They've just *sounded* the bell for our next class.	(action)
Aunt Gertrude's illness *sounds* quite mild.	(state of being)
Harry already *tasted* the soup.	(action)
These strawberries don't *taste* very sweet.	(state of being)

One difference between the state-of-being and action forms of verbs is that in a sentence with an action verb, the subject *does* something. In a sentence with a state-of-being form of the verb, the subject just is.

The mailman *weighs* the package.	(active—the mailman is doing the action: he is *weighing* the package)
The package *weighs* ten pounds.	(state of being—the package can't do anything; its weight always stays the same)

c. Helping verbs—auxiliaries

Many tenses and other structures in English need more than just the verb. They also need another small verb to "help" form that tense or question. We call these small verbs *helping* verbs or *auxiliaries*. We use an auxiliary together with another verb (called a *full* verb). The main English auxiliaries are *be, do, have,* and *will*. Except for *will*, auxiliaries are also real verbs with their own complete meanings. But when we use a verb as an auxiliary, we only want it to help us understand the tense. The full verb gives the actual meaning of the sentence. Here are the four main auxiliaries and some of the ways we use them.

Be is used for:

- all progressive tenses—present, past, and (together with the auxiliary *will*) future

My head *is aching*.
My head *was aching* all morning.
My head *will be aching* tomorrow.

- the negative form of all progressive tenses

My head *isn't aching* anymore.

- the simple future tense with *going to*, including the negative form

The children *are not going to visit* their cousins tomorrow.

- questions in all the progressive tenses

Are my parents watch*ing* TV?

Do is used for:

- questions in the simple present and simple past tenses

What *does* Carol *study* every afternoon?
Do these buses *stop* at the library?
Did Meg *telephone* you this afternoon?

Will is used for:

- the simple future and simple future progressive tenses

Who _will_ pay for the wedding gift?
The movie _will_ be starting in five minutes.

- the negative form of the simple future and simple future progressive tenses

Tom _won't_ ride the bus to work.
I _won't_ eat any meat except chicken.

- questions in all the simple future and simple future progressive tenses

When _will_ Mike clean his room?
Will John buy a new car this year?
Will Karen take the Concorde to Paris?

Have is used for:

- all *perfect tenses*—present, past, and (together with the auxiliary *will*) future (see Chapter 7, section a; *Other verb tenses—the perfect tenses*)

I *have eaten.*
I *had eaten.*
I *will have eaten.*

d. Basic verb tenses—the present, the past, the future

There are three basic categories of tenses in English: the present, the past, and the future.

THE BASICS

- *Present tenses* show what is happening at or near the moment we are speaking (usually, but not always, "now").

I *am reading* a good book now.

The Wilsons *are having* a party on Saturday.

The play *is ending* today.

- *Past tenses* show what happened in the past, and the actions or events are completely finished at the moment we are speaking.

Terry and Joan *left* on their honeymoon last week. (leave)

Mother *visited* me yesterday, and we *ate* lunch at a restaurant. (visit/eat)

Ingrid *graduated* from the Sorbonne before she *came* to the United States. (graduate/come)

- *Future tenses* show what we plan to do or expect *will* happen but have not yet happened by the time we are speaking.

I *will take* Bill to the doctor tomorrow.

Harry and Yvonne *are going to build* a new house next year.

Mona *won't speak to* her husband until he apologizes. (won't = will not)

There are also perfect tenses that start in the past, but continue into the present or, sometimes, the future. See Chapter 7, section a; *Other verb tenses—the perfect tenses* for examples.

e. Simple and progressive verb forms

Each of the tenses described in section d has three forms: simple, progressive, and perfect. You will learn all about the perfect tenses in Chapter 7. Here, we will focus on the simple and progressive forms.

Simple tenses: These include the *simple present, simple past,* and *simple future* (this has two forms—*will* and *be going to*). All simple tenses talk about complete actions. These are often short actions or an action we do regularly.

Progressive tenses: These include the *present progressive*, *past progressive*, and *future progressive*. Progressive tenses always talk about *continuous* actions. The actions may be happening as we speak ("now"—the *present* progressive), or the action may go from one past point in time to another past point (the *past progressive*), or the verb form may describe a continuous action that will begin and end in the future (the *future* progressive).

Simple Present Tense

The simple present tense is the same as the verb's dictionary form, but changes slightly if the subject is *he*, *she*, or *it* by adding *-s* (or *-es*, depending on the spelling of the verb) in the simple present. The verbs *be, do,* and *have* are the only exceptions.

We use this tense to talk about:

- regular actions or habits (these actions may be daily, hourly, or just frequently)

Eric usually *drinks* his coffee with milk.
The last bus to Hartford *leaves* at 6:45.
My cats always *play* wildly from 11:00 p.m. until morning.
I don't *put* butter on bread.
Martin *works* in the sales department.

- scientific or mathematical facts

Asbestos *causes* lung cancer.
Kiwi fruit *contains* more vitamin C than an orange.
Six times six *equals* thirty-six.

- things most people agree are "true," or general statements

Water *expands* when frozen.
Normal body temperature *is* 98.6° F.
Warm air *rises*.

- states of being such as feelings or thoughts

Jenny *doesn't forget* kind behavior.
My friends *envy* my long hair.
Charles *worries* about everything.

Simple Past Tense

The simple past tense usually adds *-ed* to the simple form of regular (and many irregular) verbs. Irregular verbs change in many different ways in the past tense. There are no changes for *he, she,* or *it* in any past tense.

We use this tense to talk about:

- completed actions or situations (often brief) that began and ended in the past

John and Kathy *went* on vacation last week.
Jim *caught* a really large trout in the river last summer.
William and I *saw* a great movie on the plane.

- a frequent action or situation in the past, or a habit that did not continue into the present

Jack *drank* espresso after dinner every night in Rome.

I *slept* until 11:00 every morning in college.

This restaurant *served* wonderful pizza before *it changed ownership.*

Simple Future Tense

There are two forms of the simple future tense. One is with the auxiliary *will.* The other is with *be* and *going to.* The two forms are often, but not always, completely interchangeable.

We use the *will* form to talk about:

- something we guess will happen, or will probably happen

The train *will be* late—it always is.

Gas prices *will start rising* again this summer.

Mother *will* probably *make* her apple pie again this Thanksgiving.

- future decisions without planning, or last-minute changes of plan

I think we *will visit* the museum tomorrow instead of today.

Oh! Dan and Sylvia *will come* with us to the theater tonight.

- a strong purpose, or the speaker's strong statement

Tommy *will get* the spelling prize next year.

I *will fight* the court's decision.

- a future plan or promise, such as a party or business meeting

Andrew and I *will bring* the wine, as I promised.
We *will arrive* at the cabin by 3:00 p.m.

- something we want someone to do for us, or something we agreed to do

Of course, Marie *will make* all the reservations.
Will you *be* one of my bridesmaids?

We use the *be going to* form to talk about:

- something we are quite sure will happen because of logic, not feelings

This *isn't going to be* an easy test.
This stock *is going to lose* value during the year.

- definite plans like business appointments, etc.

Sara *is going to get* her checkup next Tuesday morning.
The board of directors *is going to meet* Friday.

- plans for the immediate or distant future

Bernard *is going to vacation* in Aruba next year.
We *are* finally *going to buy* a computer.

Present Progressive

All progressive tenses use some form of the auxiliary *be* and add *-ing* to the verb.

We use this tense to talk about:

- something that is happening "now"

Joe *is taking* a shower at the moment.
We *are getting dressed* now.

- an event in the immediate future—often one particular event

I'*m moving* into my new house this weekend.
Charles and Betty *are driving* to Boston for Memorial Day.

- a temporary situation that may continue for a while, but will not become a daily routine

They *are rebuilding* the house after the fire.
Chris *is working* eighteen hours a day on this project.

- A situation that happens often—usually with bad results—but that may not be happening "now"

Sam *is having* money problems again.
Marilyn *is getting* her second divorce.
Cheryl *is having* another facelift.

THE BASICS

Past Progressive

We form the past progressive with the *past tense* of the auxiliary be (*was/were*) and add *-ing* to the verb. The only exception is *was/were going to* and the dictionary form of the verb (*I was going to visit you in the hospital last month.*). We use this form to show an incomplete or interrupted plan in the past. The difference between the past progressive and the simple past is that the past progressive talks about a *continuing* action from one point in the past to another point, still in the past. This means that we can use it only with longer actions or situations. We can also use it with *while* and a second verb in either the past progressive or simple past to show two actions happening at the same time (*June was singing while Stuart was trying to read the paper.*).

We use this tense to talk about:

- past events that continued from one point in the past to a closer point that is also in the past

The cat *was meowing* from 7:00 p.m. until dawn.

Our air-conditioner *was not working* for more than three weeks last summer.

- a particular moment during a continuing action

Mary *was getting* a beautiful suntan; then a heavy thunderstorm began.

- events leading up to the main action of a story

The policeman *was* just *opening* the car door when I started to explain the mistake.

- something that happened one time, but included a repeated action.

The man was so angry, he *was pulling* his hair out!

- an action that was incomplete or interrupted

The baby *was* just *spilling* his juice when I picked him up.

Future Progressive

We form the future progressive with *will* or *be going to*, the auxiliary *be*, and the main verb with -*ing* (*Andrew* will be painting *from 10:00 to 7:00 tonight.*). The reason we use the future progressive instead of the simple future is that in English only a progressive tense can show that an action is continuing. Simple tenses give a general future time frame for an action or intention, with no beginning or ending.

We use this tense to talk about:

- an action that will be happening at a specific point, or between two specific points in the future

The traffic *will* still *be moving* slowly one hour from now.
Mother *will be resting* between now and 4:00 p.m.
Richard *will be practicing* his golf swing at the club all day Saturday.

- a planned or scheduled future action that will be in progress at the future point we are discussing

***Are* the Joneses *going to be leaving* for Kenya on the 27th?**
Phillip *is going to be getting* a haircut at 11:00 tomorrow morning.

THE BASICS

- an action we expect will be continuing at a future time

Tina *will be enjoying* her maternity leave at home next month.

- the listener's plans for a future point in time

***Who will be running* your department after you become general manager next month?**

f. Contractions with verbs

In conversation, it is natural for English speakers to make the two sounds of the pronoun and the auxiliary (or the main verb) into one sound. This is called a contraction. In this way, *I am* becomes *I'm*. We mainly use these *contractions* in conversation, but they are also popular in informal written English. Here are some English contractions.

- contractions with *be/has:*

I am	= I'm
you are	= you're
he is/he has	= he's
she is/she has	= she's
it is	= it's*
we are	= we're
they are	= they're

Note: * Remember that *it's*, the contraction of *it is*, has a different meaning from *its*, the possessive form of *it*.

TALKING ABOUT ACTIONS AND BEING

- negative contractions with *be:*

is not	**= isn't**
are not	**= aren't**
was not	**= wasn't**
were not	**= weren't**

- contractions with *will:*

I will	**= I'll**
you will	**= you'll**
he will	**= he'll**
she will	**= she'll**
it will	**= it'll**
we will	**= we'll**
they will	**= they'll**

- negative contractions with *will:*

will not = won't

- contractions with *have/is:*

I have	**= I've**
you have	**= you've**
he has/he is	**= he's**
she has/she is	**= she's**
it has/it is	**= it's**
we have	**= we've**
they have	**= they've**

THE BASICS

- negative contractions with *have:*

do not have	**= don't have***
does not have	**= doesn't have**
have not	**= haven't***
has not	**= hasn't**
had not	**= hadn't**

Note: * Be careful to keep these meanings separate:

don't/doesn't have = not have (own) a car, a house, etc.
have/has/had not = negative form of auxiliary *have*, used to form perfect tenses

- negative contractions with *do**/does/did:*

do not	**= don't**
does not	**= doesn't**
did not	**= didn't**

Note: ** There are only negative contractions for *do*; there are no affirmative contractions.

3 | Making Statements; Asking and Answering Questions

a. The basic English sentence

A complete English sentence must have at least two things: a subject and a verb. The subject shows who is doing the "action" (or thinking the thought, or feeling the emotion); the verb shows what the action, thought, feeling, or situation is. Of course, even a simple sentence can have much more than a subject and verb, but it must have those two things.

The word order in an English sentence is very strict in most cases. In a statement, the subject comes first, followed by the verb (or helping verb + main verb). *

The dog is barking.
  (s) (hv) (v)
Snow falls in January.
  (s)   (v)
Margaret is sleeping.
  (s)   (hv) (v)

* (s) = subject; (hv) = helping verb; (v) = main verb.

A sentence usually has some other parts as well. Most sentences have an object—the part of the sentence that the subject "does" something to. The object, usually a noun or a phrase, often "receives" the action (or the effect of the action or thought). The object always follows the main verb in the sentence, but it doesn't always come immediately after the verb. Sometimes, it comes after a preposition. In the following sentences, the subject is underlined once, and the object is underlined twice.

THE BASICS

Joan writes cookbooks.

Horses eat grass.

My cats chase mice all day.

Linda drinks coffee at breakfast.

Martin gave a ring to Erica.

Our house has a balcony.

James drives his car every day.

The grocery store is next to the hardware store.

The toy store is in the mall.

In most sentences, we need to give a little more detail, so we use certain words (*adjectives* and *adverbs*) to describe the noun(s) or verb(s) in the sentence. Adjectives describe nouns—their shape, color, the way they look or feel (the *round* window, the *yellow* house, the *pretty* girl, the *angry* driver), etc. Many adverbs describe verbs—the way the subject does the action (he drives *carefully*, she danced *well*, she walked *slowly*). You will learn more about these words in Chapter 4.

b. Making statements

There are two types of statements. You can confirm that an action, situation, thought, or event has happened or is happening (*I speak English*). This is called an *affirmative* statement. Or you can deny those things (*I don't speak Chinese*) with a *negative* statement.

Affirmative statements follow the "typical" English word order: subject, verb, object:

It's three o'clock.

I have a dog.*

Joan is a good cook.

Dave and George work in the Accounting Department.

Bob is watching a baseball game.

We're going to eat shrimp tonight.

My children can play the piano.

Note: * When we use *have* as a main verb (meaning "own," "belong to," "is part of," or as part of a phrase—"I *have* a headache"), we don't contract it to *I've/he's/they've,* etc. When we use *have* as a helping verb—usually to form one of the perfect tenses (see Chapter 2, section a, *Verbs—all about time*)—we usually do contract it to *I've/he's/they've,* etc.

He's been to Paris three times.

Negative statements also follow the "typical" English word order, but add a negative—usually one of the helping verbs (see Chapter 2, section c. *Helping verbs—auxiliaries*) + *not.* The word order then becomes: subject, helping verb, negative, (main) verb, object:

without auxiliary	**with auxiliary**
I'*m not* tired.**	The Donalssons *don't* live at this address now.
That *isn't* my car.	
Maureen *isn't* Irish.	We *aren't* having steak for dinner.
Mark *wasn't* at the party.	I *won't* invite her to dinner.
	Sheila and I *can't* visit you until Christmas.

Note: ** *I am not* is always contracted to *I'm not.* "I amn't" is incorrect.

c. Yes/no questions

There are several types of questions in English. The two main types are "simple" questions (questions the listener can answer with "yes" or "no") and those using "question words" (such as *what, when, where, who,* and *why*). When we ask simple questions, the usual word order changes. Instead of the subject-verb-object order of statements, the helping verb moves to the beginning of the sentence, just before the subject.

THE BASICS

Affirmative statement:	**He *is* driving.**
Negative statement:	**He *isn't* driving.**
Question:	***Is* he driving?**

The helping verb we use to make the question depends on the tense of the sentence (see Chapter 2, sections d and e, *Basic verb tenses* and *Simple and progressive verb forms*).

Simple present:	***Do*** **you drive?**
	Does **she drive?**
Simple past:	***Did*** **you drive?**
Simple future:	***Will*** **you drive?/*Are* you going to drive?**
Present progressive:	***Am*** **I driving?**
	Is **she driving?**
	Are **you driving?**
Past progressive:	***Was*** **she driving?**
	Were **you driving?**
Future progressive:	***Will*** **you be driving? /*Are* you going to be driving?**

d. Short answers

It is most common in English, especially with yes/no questions, to give short answers. Like statements, short answers can be either affirmative (*Yes, it is*) or negative (*No, it's not/No, it isn't*). The form the short answer takes depends on which helping verb the main verb uses. The tense of the sentence decides which helping verb you must use in the short form answers. Here are some examples.

- Simple present uses *do/does* except when the main verb is *be*. This also includes *there is/there are* (see section g, *There is/there are*). We use *be* as a helping verb only in progressive tenses.

Do you work here?	→→→	Yes, I *do.*/ No, I *don't.*
Does John have black hair?	→→→	Yes, he *does.*/ No, he *doesn't.*
Do Mary and Lew speak Spanish?	→→→	Yes, they *do.*/ No, they *don't.*
Is this a Japanese coin?	→→→	Yes, it *is.**/ No, it *isn't.* *
Are the children in school now?	→→→	Yes, they *are.**/ No, they *aren't.*
Is there a bank near here?	→→→	Yes, *there is.**/ No, *there isn't.*
Are there mice in the attic?	→→→	Yes, *there are.*/ No, *there aren't.*
Do you have a match?	→→→	Yes, I *do.*/ No, I *don't.*
	OR	Yes, I *have.**/ No, I *haven't.*
Does Paula have pets?	→→→	Yes, she *does.*/ No, she *doesn't.*
	OR	Yes, she *has.**/ No, she *hasn't.*

Note: * With short answers, we never contract these verbs in the affirmative, *only* in the negative.

• Simple past uses *did/didn't* except when the main verb is *be* (including *there was/there were*—see section g, *There is/there are*).

Did you walk here?	→→→	Yes, I *did.*/ No, I *didn't.*
Did the Logans sell their house?	→→→	Yes, they *did.*/ No, they *didn't.*
Was the dinner good?	→→→	Yes, it *was.*/ No, it *wasn't.*

THE BASICS

Were Tim and Vicky happy?	→→→	Yes, they *were.*/ No, they *weren't.**
Was there a lot of snow in Detroit?	→→→	Yes, there *was.*/ No, there *wasn't.*
Were there seats for the concert?	→→→	Yes, there *were.*/ No, there *weren't.**

Note: * Don't confuse *were* (past tense form of *are*; pronounced "werr") with *we're* (contraction of *we are*; pronounced "weer").

The Logans *were* in Puerto Rico last year.

We *were* eating breakfast from 7:00 to 7:30.

There *were* enough biscuits for all the guests.

We're from San Francisco, but now we live in Chicago.

- Simple future uses *will/won't* (or *am-is-are going to/am not-isn't-aren't going to*). This also includes *there will/there won't be; there is/there isn't going to be* (see section g, *There is/there are*).

Will you go to the seminar?	→→→	Yes, I *will.*/ No, I *won't.*
Will Dan take a bus to the beach?	→→→	Yes, he *will.*/ No, he *won't.*
Will the hotel be expensive?	→→→	Yes, it *will.*/ No, it *won't.*
Will the dogs have enough water?	→→→	Yes, they *will.*/ No, they *won't.**
Will there be music at the party?	→→→	Yes, there *will.*/ No, there *won't.*

OR

Are you going to go to the seminar?	→→→	Yes, I *am*./ No, I'm *not*.
Is Dan going to take a bus to the beach?	→→→	Yes, he *is*./ No, he's *not*. / No, he *isn't*.**
Is the hotel going to be expensive?	→→→	Yes, it *is*./ No, it's *not*./ No, it *isn't*.**
Are the dogs going to have enough water?	→→→	Yes, they *are*./ No, they're *not*./ No, they *aren't*.**
Is there going to be music at the party?	→→→	Yes, there *is*./ No, there *isn't*.

Note: * With short answers, we never contract *will* in the affirmative, *only* in the negative.

        ** Either form can be used, but only with the contractions as they are shown.

- Present progressive uses *be* as the helping verb (*am-is-are/am not-isn't-aren't*). There is no progressive form in any tense for *there is/there are; there isn't/there aren't* (see section g, *There is/there are*).

Are you working now?	→→→	Yes, I *am*./ No, I'm *not*.
Is Mike watching the ballgame?	→→→	Yes, he *is*./ No, he's *not*./ No, he *isn't*.***
Are Harry and Susie swimming in the pool?	→→→	Yes, they *are*./ No, they're *not*./ No, they *aren't*. ***

53

Is Tony being a good boy?	→→→	Yes, he *is.*/
		No, he *isn't.*/
		No, he's *not*. ***
Is your back still hurting?	→→→	Yes, it *is.*/
		No, it *isn't.*/
		No, it's *not*. ***
Are the children being noisy?	→→→	Yes, they *are.*/
		No, they're *not.*/
		No, they *aren't*. ***

Note: *** Either form can be used, but only with the contractions as they are shown.

- Past progressive uses the past tense of *be* as the helping verb (*was/were; wasn't/weren't*). There is no progressive form in any tense for *there was/there were; there wasn't/there weren't* (see section g, *There is/there are*).

Were you sleeping just now?	→→→	Yes, I *was.*/
		No, I *wasn't*.
Was Sandra playing golf on Friday morning?	→→→	Yes, she *was.*/
		No, she *wasn't*.
Were the helicopters flying over our house at 6:30?	→→→	Yes, they *were.*/
		No, they *weren't*.

If you don't use the contraction (*wasn't/weren't*), the short answer may sound emphatic or angry.

| Were you crying when I opened the door? | →→→ | No, I was not! |
| Were John's parents rich? | →→→ | No, they certainly were not. |

- Future progressive uses *will/won't be* (or *am-is-are going to be/am not-isn't-aren't going to be*) as the helping verb. There is no progressive form in any tense for *there will/there won't be; there is/there isn't going to be* (see section g, *There is/there are*).

54

Will you be attending the lecture tomorrow?	→→→	Yes, I *will.*/ No, I *won't.*
Will Ralph be taking his vacation next week?	→→→	Yes, he *will.*/ No, he *won't.*
Will the sales managers be using this room during the morning?	→→→	Yes, they *will.*/ No, they *won't.*
Is the hotel going to be expensive?	→→→	Yes, it *is.*/ No, it's *not.*/ No, it *isn't.**

OR

Are you going to be attending the lecture tomorrow?	→→→	Yes, I *am.*/ No, I'm *not.*
Is Ralph going to be taking his vacation next week?	→→→	Yes, he *is.*/ No, he's *not.* / No, he *isn't.**
Are the sales managers going to be using this room during the morning?	→→→	Yes, they *are.*/ No, they're *not.*/ No, they *aren't.**

Note: * The same rules about contractions apply to short answers in the future progressive as in the simple future.

We will learn short answers for other forms (such as modals or perfect tenses) later in this book.

e. Full answers

You can use short answers only for yes/no questions. For other questions, especially those that start with "question words" you need to give full answers. We often use full answers even with yes/no questions when we want to add extra information. With short answers, you don't use contractions with the affirmative, but with full answers you can.

THE BASICS

- **Simple present:**

  Where do you work?
  I work downtown on Front Street.
  No, I don't./No, I don't work downtown. (I work at home.)

- **Simple past:**

  When did Elaine and Mark get married?
  They got married in February.

- **Simple future:**

  Will Louis graduate in May?
  No, he won't./No, he won't graduate in May. (He'll graduate in June.)

- **Present progressive:**

  Are you waiting for a taxi?
  Yes, I am./Yes, I'm waiting for a taxi. (I called twenty minutes ago.)
  No, I'm not./No, I'm not waiting for a taxi. (I'm waiting for the bus.)

- **Past progressive:**

  Was the lawn mower making a lot of noise?
  Yes, it was./Yes, the lawn mower was making a lot of noise (but I don't mind).
  No, it wasn't./No, the lawn mower wasn't making a lot of noise. (I wasn't home.)

- **Future progressive:**

  What will you be doing during the holidays?
  I'll be working during the holidays, but I'm going to take a vacation in January.

f. Question words—"wh-" words and more

We can't always ask yes/no questions in English. Often we need more information. If we want to get detailed information, we need to use "question words." There are several question words, and they all ask for a different kind of information. These are the most frequently used question words in English:

what	**why**
which	**how**
when	**how** (+ adjective/adverb)
who	**how many**
whose	**how much**
where	

In a basic English sentence, question words can be either the subject (_Who broke the glass?_) or the object (_Who is Marie dating?_). If the question word comes just in front of the main verb (_not_ a helping verb), then the question word is usually the subject. This is important because you can always get the same _kind_ of information from a question word, whether it is the subject or object, but you can't get the same exact answer. The sentence's word order also changes depending on the subject. If the question word is the object, you have to use the helping verb _do/be_ in the sentence, but not if the question word is the subject. Look carefully at the word order of the examples. The subject (or the pronoun that is substituting for the subject) is underlined.

Who is speaking with Betty? (subject)
Who is calling us? (object)
What happened after the game? (subject)
What taxi company does Andrew use? (object)

• What

We use this question word more than any of the others. When we use _what_ alone, we are asking for general information. We can also use _what_ in front of a noun to asks details about the subject. We also use *what* to find out the time (*What time is it?*):

What time is it?*
What are his hobbies?
What do you want to eat for dinner?
What book is Michael reading?
What kind of dog is that? (what breed)
What happened to your eye? (accident? fight?)

Note: * Asking *what time is it* will get you the exact clock time. Many native speakers use *when* instead of *what time is it.* Using *when* will usually get you a more general time, or the time of day (morning, afternoon, etc.).

What time **does the train leave?**	→→→	**It leaves at 2:07.**
When **does the train leave?**	→→→	**It leaves around 2:00.**
What time **do you usually have dinner?**	→→→	**We usually have dinner at 6:30.**
When **do you usually have dinner?**	→→→	**We usually have dinner in the early evening.**
What time **is Michael's wedding reception?**	→→→	**It starts at 1:00.**
When **is Michael's wedding reception?**	→→→	**It's next Saturday afternoon.**

- Which

Using *which* involves choosing between a small or specific group of people, animals, things, or possible events. We use *which* to get information about, or to describe, selecting one of two things.

Which way is the library?	(only a few ways to get there)
Which of your sons is better at sports?	(limited number of sons)
Which car are you taking today?	(she owns more than one car)
I have two kinds of ice cream; which would you like?	
Carla is never sure which language to speak when she visits her grandparents.	(bilingual family)
We can't decide which of the candidates to vote for.	(probably more than one candidate in a political race)
Which branch of the military was your father in?	(only four possibilities)

English speakers often use *which* and *what* as if they were interchangeable—especially in casual speech, but there is a difference. *Which* and *what* both talk about choosing between possibilities, but *what* makes the listener think of an unlimited group.

What would you like to drink?	→→→	**Which wine is your favorite?**
What colors does your husband like?	→→→	**Which of these ties will your husband like?**

• When

We use *when* if we want to get information about the *general*, rather than the precise, time something happens. (See the note after *what*.)

When is Philip's birthday? (in March, next week, on the 25th, etc.)
When will we get your check?
When is Easter this year?

When are you going to visit us?

When did we buy this house?

When does the new sales assistant start work?

- Who

We use *who* if we want to get information about a person (or even several people). We never use *who* to talk about animals— not even domestic pets with names. Instead, we use *what*. We can use *who* to get the actual name of a person (or a business), or it can give a more general description. If you really want a name, you can ask *what is his/her name* instead.

Who are those people?	
Who is that woman over there?	
Who won the Best Actor Oscar?	
Who does your hair?	(what is the name of your hairdresser)
Who's going to help me wash the dishes?*	(parent speaking to his/her family)
Who's calling, please?	(please give me your name; used for telephone calls only)

Note: * *Who's* (*who* + *is*) is generally the only contraction with *who* that most people use. In casual or rapid spoken (*not* written) English, *who're* (*who* + *are*) is used by some people. Because *who's* and *whose* are pronounced the same way, even some native speakers confuse them in writing—be careful.

- Whose

We use *whose* to get information about the "owner" of something if the subject is a thing or an animal. Sometimes, we also use *whose* to get the name of the person who made an item— an artist, a dress designer, a writer, etc.

Whose house is that gray one?

Whose cake recipe is this—Aunt Ellen's?

Those dogs aren't Tony's—whose are they?

Whose gloves did Paula take by accident?

Lovely dress—whose is it? Lagerfeldt's?

Whose style is Brad copying—Hemingway's or Raymond Chandler's?

- Where

We use *where* to get information about the place that an action or event happens or a location we are trying to find. We use *where* most often to find an object we are looking for.

Where is my hairbrush?

Where are Tom's parents living now?

Where is State Street?

Where do you live?

Where does this train stop next?

Where did the committee decide to have the dinner party?

Where is the nearest bank, please?

- Why

We use *why* to find out the cause of an action or event, or the reason behind a person's actions. Often, but not always, the answers we get use the word *because* (see Chapter 7, section c, *Connecting things* and *thoughts*).

Why did you do this?

Why are you crying?

Why is Charlie going to quit his job?

Why are the company's sales so bad?

Why does Elaine want to marry that man?

THE BASICS

In casual speech, some people may use *what . . . for* instead of *why* to ask the reasoning behind an action or choice.

What did you use the special china for?	→→→	**Why did you use the special china?**
What did you go to the store for?	→→→	**Why did you go to the store?**

Why do I feel so alone!*
Why are people so cruel sometimes?*

Note: *We often use *why* in this type of general, philosophical "question" that we don't really expect anyone to answer (see Chapter 10, section c, *Rhetorical questions*).

• How

Not all question words start with *wh-*. *How* is often used to get information about the way a person did (or should do) something—especially in a learning situation. *How* is also used to show surprise that a person was able to do something very difficult.

How can I get to the stock exchange, please?
How do I change the screen color on this computer?
How did you find your way back home?
How is Eva able to look so young?
How did Paul pay for our tickets?
How will Agnes find the money for all that dental work?

• How + adjective/adverb

We also use *how* with an adjective or adverb (see Chapter 4, *Describing Things*) to find out information about the degree or level of a situation, or to get facts of some kind.

How severe was the earthquake in Mexico? (degree of damage)
How big is the living room? (measurement)
How bad does your father feel today? (level of illness)
How soon is Mary going to graduate? (how much time)
How often does it rain in this area? (how many times per month/year)
How long is this movie? (how many hours)

In Chapter 6, *Talking About Quantities*, we will study in detail the two categories of nouns: *mass-count* nouns—those nouns that already stand for a quantity and so don't add *-s* or have any real plural form (*sand, wine, money, water*, etc.)—and *countable* nouns—those nouns, the most common ones, that we can add an *-s* or other plural ending to (*books, dogs, children, shelves*, etc.).

The question words *how many* and *how much* are used to talk about the number or amount of *countable* and *mass-count* nouns.

- How many

We use *how many* to get information about the number of *countable* nouns.

How many books does Andrew read each year?
How many wives did Henry VIII have?
How many children attend Sarah's reading class?

- How much

We use *how much* to get information about the amount of *mass-count* nouns.

How much does this car cost?/How much is this car? (money/price)
How much water can you drink?
How much time does Albert spend at the office every week?
How much pain do you feel in this hand? (degree of pain)

THE BASICS

g. There is/there are

When we want to talk about something for the first time, to agree on the details of a thing or a situation, we use the words *there is* or *there are*. We use *there is* when we talk about a single noun (or with mass-count nouns), and we use *there are* with plural forms of countable nouns. We usually contract *there is* to *there's*, but we don't contract *there are* to "*there're*" except in very quickly spoken, casual English.

There's a crack in the wall.

There's a fly in this soup!

I think *there's* one sandwich left.

Look, *there's* water running down the stairs!

There's a glass of milk in the kitchen.

There are three phone messages for you.

There are two boys playing on our lawn.

There are dozens of people waiting to get into the restaurant.

The negative forms of *there is* (depending on the sentence) are *there isn't* and *there's no*. The negative is almost always contracted. The negative forms of *there are* are *there aren't* and *there are no*.

Because the verb *be* is part of *there is/there are*, we use these words in all the same simple (*not* progressive) tense forms as *be*.

---

there is
there was
there will be
there's going to be

there are
there were
there will be
there are going to be

Here are forms of the perfect tenses (see Chapter 7, section a, *Other verb tenses—the perfect tenses*).

there has been
there had been
there will have been
there have been
there had been
there will have been

We use *there is/there are* in the following situations:

- to talk about something we have just noticed, or that we (but not the listener) can see

Look, there's that book you wanted!
Is there a spot on the carpet?
Oh, there's a run in my new pantyhose!
There are my friends Joe and Bob crossing the street.

- to give the listener some news or information, often facts or instructions

There's a button on the CD-player to repeat a song track.
There are several articles about crime in the newspaper today.
There are clean towels and sheets for you in this closet.

- to ask for general information

Is there a drugstore around here?
Are there buses that go downtown?
Do you know if there's a bank in this mall?
I wonder if there's a used book store in this town.
Will there be beach towels available by the pool?

- to begin a conversation about a subject

There are several famous homes around Nashville, you know.
There's a wonderful restaurant just around the corner from here.
There was an old painting in the Louvre that looked exactly like mother.
Oh, yes, there's something I wanted to discuss with you.

- to describe something that we have heard or read

I've heard that there's not much cholesterol in eggs.
People said there was a lot of crime in this neighborhood in the 1980s.
The paper reports that there are ten health clubs for every thousand residents in Los Angeles.

- to list quantities of things or people

There's no brandy left, but there's a bottle of rum and there are two or three kinds of liqueur in that cabinet.
There are only two suitcases in the baggage claim.

There will be a reception at 6:00, dinner at 7:00, and coffee in the library at 8:30.

There are four items in my cart: a loaf of bread, a bag of apples, and two kinds of cheese.

There have been six job applicants today: five for the sales position and one for the marketing job.

English speakers use *there is/there are* to talk about things for the first time in a conversation, not when continuing to talk about them in detail.

There are seven children in the class.	→→→	**They are all bilingual.** (they = the children in the class)
There are a few bottles of champagne in the refrigerator.	→→→	**But they aren't French.** (they = the bottles of champagne)
There is an article about the president's trip in the newspaper.	→→→	**It talks about his schedule.** (it = the article)
There's a gas station at the next corner.	→→→	**It opens in ten minutes.** (it = the gas station)

Describing Things

a. Describing nouns—simple adjectives

Most people like to describe the subjects of their sentences in some detail, instead of just naming the noun(s). If we say *a dog*, or *the dog*, or *my dog*, it's not always enough, so we need a way to describe the dog in detail, either in individual situations or in a general way. To do that, we use *adjectives*—words that describe nouns. After nouns and verbs, adjectives are the words we use most often in English sentences.

If you say "a boat," you aren't telling the listener much about the boat. If you say "*a beautiful, big, shiny, new, white sail*boat," the listener understands all about that particular boat. All the words between *a* and *boat* are adjectives.

To confirm that a word is an adjective, always ask yourself if it tells you what the noun is like—is it beautiful or ugly, clean or dirty, long or short, new or old, black or white, hard or soft, etc. If the word gives you that information, it's an adjective. English adjectives don't have tenses and don't change form.

As you know, in English word order, the subject comes before the verb (see Chapter 3, section a, *The basic English sentence*). We put adjectives in two places. About 90 percent of all adjectives come just before the noun they describe (which isn't *always* the subject of the sentence, although it often is).

that *expensive* ring

a *beautiful* day

five *active* children

the *eager* student

those *noisy* dogs

Sometimes, if the verb following the subject is *be*, *become*, or *get* (or a few other verbs like *look, seem,* etc.), an adjective can also follow the verb.

Alex is *blond*.
Our table is *antique*.
This month's electric bill was *high*.
Does he seem *happy*?
Sandra looks *pretty* in blue.

Most adjectives can go in either place, depending on the sentence—often without much, or any, change in the meaning of the sentence.

My *new* car is a Lincoln.	→→→	The Lincoln is *new*.
Tommy lost his *expensive* watch.	→→→	Tommy's watch was *expensive*.
Thank you for the *delicious* cake, Anna.	→→→	Anna's cakes are always *delicious*.
Brenda has *talented* children.	→→→	Brenda's children are *talented*.
We've had very *strange* weather lately.	→→→	Lately, the weather has been very *strange*.

A small group of adjectives can come only before the noun, not after the verb. Some of these are *indoor, outdoor, countless, only, main, principal, existing, former, previous, occasional.*

correct:	**The *existing* bridge is narrow.**
incorrect:	**The bridge is *existing* and narrow.**
correct:	**This is the *main* office.**
incorrect:	**This office is *main*.**

correct:	**There were *countless* traffic accidents.**
	(too many to count)
incorrect:	**The traffic accidents were *countless*.**

correct:	**Veronica has an *indoor* pool.**
incorrect:	**Veronica's pool is *indoor*.**

We can often use adjectives after "nonaction" verbs (*state-of-being* verbs—see Chapter 2, section b, *Types of verbs*), especially *perception verbs*—verbs that describe feelings or one of the five physical senses. On the other hand, we seldom use adjectives after action verbs.

That bath <u>felt</u> *good*.
The new carpet <u>looks</u> *lovely*.
Your bread <u>smells</u> *delicious*.
Harry's cough <u>sounds</u> *serious*.
My fish <u>tastes</u> *strange*.

There are also a few adjectives that we don't use in front of nouns. This type of adjective often talks about a person's feelings, including physical health. Some of these are *ill, well, alive, asleep, awake, aware, glad, pleased, alone, apart, afraid, ashamed, upset, annoyed.*

correct:	**My boss is *annoyed*.**	
incorrect:	**My *annoyed* boss.**	(my *angry* boss)

correct:	**My son is *well*.**	
incorrect:	**My *well* son.**	(my *healthy* son)

correct:	**His wife was *upset*.**	
incorrect:	**His *upset* wife.**	(his *distressed* wife)

correct:	**The dog seemed *afraid*.**	
incorrect:	**The *afraid* dog.**	(the *frightened/fearful* dog)

correct:	**The child was *asleep*.**	
incorrect:	**The *asleep* child.**	(the *sleeping* child)

The postion of an adjective within a question is very important.

correct:	**Is this watch old?**
incorrect:	**Is old this watch?**

correct:	**How expensive is it?**
incorrect:	**How is it expensive?**

Because there are many different ways to describe a noun, and many different things about a noun that we notice, there are also many different categories of adjectives.

If you look at each of the examples, you can see that the same kinds of adjectives always come in the same place. In English, if there are two or more different kinds of adjectives that describe the same noun, the adjectives follow a definite order. Here are some adjectives in each category, and the order they come in.

• Impression

Any adjective that gives an observation comes ahead of one that states a fact: *The writer's <u>skillful</u>, <u>brief</u> descriptions. . . ."* *Skillful* is the speaker's opinion; it's a fact that the writer's descriptions are *brief*.

It was a *marvelous* play.
What a *wonderful* dinner!

This book is *fascinating*.
That movie was *thrilling*.
She has such a *beautiful* face.
The doctor has a *relaxing*, professional manner.

- Size

Any fact adjective always comes after, never in front of, opinion adjectives. Among fact adjectives, size always comes first, followed by shape, temperature, and age.

The company has *huge* debts and very *small* cash reserves.
Ben drives a *low*, streamlined, bright red sports car.
My diet allows me only a *tiny* amount of food.
Those *short* skirts are fashionable again.

- Shape/temperature

An item's or person's shape or other physical description always follows size, but always comes before age. Temperature also comes before age.

She had a pleasant, *round-cheeked* face and a trim figure.
The *spacious, high-ceilinged,* freezing rooms depressed her.
The *steaming hot*, fresh bread tasted wonderful.

- Age

In this first group of fact adjectives, age always comes last.

The plump, smiling, *young* child played in the garden.
My dear, loyal, *fourteen-year-old* terrier died last winter.
Please hand me that *antique* music box over there.
Our sturdy *old* Volvo is beginning to have mechanical problems.

- Color

The second group of fact adjectives start with color. If there are two *separate, equal* colors in a noun, we use *and* between the two colors (in *black and white*, for example, *black* always comes first). If the colors mix in equal parts to make a new color, we use a hyphen between them. If one color influences the other color without changing it, the first color adjective will often end in *-ish, -y,* or *-like.*

Jeanette had beautiful *reddish-gold* hair.

His *blue-gray* eyes sparkled.

The *red, white,* and *blue* flag waved in the breeze.

The child's teeth were *pearly white.*

- Nationality (people)/place or origin (things)

Adjectives describing nationality, or the place that something came from, always come after the noun's color.

We had a lovely black *Chinese* table in the hall.

There were many *Italian* and *French* fashion magazines in the waiting room.

Zachary loved to drive *British* sports cars.

- Style

When we talk about things, especially in history, art, architecture, or fashion, we use words to describe the style—*Victorian, Impressionist*, etc. These style adjectives come after color adjectives, but before material adjectives.

Mona had an unfashionable, *pre-Raphaelite* beauty.

The small, ancient, *XVII-dynasty* paintings came from a pharaoh's tomb.

Ann loves expensive, elaborate, Italian *baroque* furniture.

• Material/type

The adjectives describing the material (*metallic, wooden, ceramic,* etc.) that something is made from come last before the noun. If the noun is a concept or situation (a *crisis, happiness, negotiations,* etc.), the adjectives describing it also come just before it.

The old, coppery, Thai *teakwood* floor was smooth as glass.

The delicate, violet-gray *silk* suited her well.

Emily's long tables were set with fine, old, Edwardian *silver* forks and knives.

The long *military* conflict became worse.

It was a *fleeting* kind of happiness. (fleeting = quickly over)

The complex, three-year *merger* negotiations ended successfully.

---

b. Describing verbs—"-ly" adverbs

There are many different types of adverbs. The largest group of them are "*-ly*" *adverbs* (also called *adverbs of manner*). Adjectives describe what something is like; adverbs describe how we *do* something. Adjectives tell us details about nouns, but adverbs give us details about verbs. Adverbs—at least *-ly* adverbs—are easy to recognize: If you ask yourself what happens in a particular sentence, or how (the *manner* in which) the action is done, the adverb will give you the answer. Adverbs tell you if the subject acted politely or rudely, did his/her work patiently or carelessly, drove recklessly or cautiously, played golf badly or skillfully, spoke to his/her children angrily or kindly, behaved or spoke happily or sadly, etc. Adjectives, on the other hand, tell the listener some part of what a specific noun *is*, not what it does.

These adverbs of manner are developed from adjectives with similar, not always identical, meanings. Most (not all) adverbs of manner are formed by adding *-ly* to the adjective. Often more than just the spelling changes, so be careful of those adverbs that have a different meaning than the adjective forms.

Helen has a *beautiful* voice.	→→→	She sang that song *beautifully*.
Bob is *enthusiastic* about his new job.	→→→	He spoke about it *enthusiastically*.
Steve always wears *expensive* clothes.	→→→	Steve always dresses *expensively*.
Frank's German is *fluent*.	→→→	Frank speaks German *fluently*.
Dad is *angry* with his neighbor.	→→→	Dad was speaking *angrily* with his neighbor last week.

Several spelling changes occur when you add *-ly* to adjectives to form *-ly* adverbs:

-ic →→→ *-ally* (basic, basic<u>ally</u>, fantastic<u>ally</u>, etc.)

-l →→→ *-lly* (beautiful, beautiful<u>ly</u>, awful<u>ly</u>, etc.)

-le →→→ *-ly* (humble, humb<u>ly</u>, terrib<u>ly</u>, etc.)

-y →→→ *-ily* (noisy, nois<u>ily</u>, thrift<u>ily</u>, etc.)

Some adjectives change meaning when they become adverbs. Here are some traps you should be careful to avoid.

The train's arriving *shortly*.	(= soon)
BUT	
The train stopped *briefly*.	(= for a *short* time)
Gene studied *hard*.	(= intensely)
BUT	
Gene *hardly* studied.	(= very small degree)
I walked *near* my old house today.	(= close to)
BUT	
I was *nearly* late for work.	(= almost)

THE BASICS

We can usually put -ly adverbs in two different places in a sentence: at the end of a sentence (*Michael drank his coffee quickly*) or between the subject and the main verb (*Michael quickly drank his coffee*). We can't put an adverb between a verb and that verb's object (*Michael drank quickly his coffee*). If the sentence is very basic—if it has no object—the adverb goes directly after the verb (*Michael spoke quickly*).

A few adverbs and adjectives are spelled and pronounced identically, but it's important to understand the difference between them because each one has a different job to do in the sentence. Here are some of those adverbs: *better, early, late, fast, straight, hard, high, low, right, wrong, free, long.* You can recognize the adjective forms if they come just before a noun or after a verb like *be* or *become.* The adverb, however, always follows a verb or a verb phrase (*get out of the car, answer the phone,* and *cook dinner* are all verb phrases).

adjective: **This is a *better* movie than last week's.**
adverb: **Paula sings *better* than Marie.**

adjective: **We watched the *early* news before dinner.**
adverb: **I'm going to go to bed *early*.**

adjective: **Linda's a *fast* worker.**
adverb: **Linda works very *fast*.**

adjective: **Studying to be a lawyer is *hard* work.**
adverb: **I'm studying *hard* for the exam.**

adjective: **There's a *late* movie on TV tonight.**
adverb: **Steve always leaves for the office a few minutes *late*.**

adjective: **This is a *long* book.**
adverb: **Writing letters takes too *long*.**

adjective: **I can't draw a *straight* line.**
adverb: **Tonight I'm going *straight* to bed.**

In questions, the adverb follows the verb.

Was he driving recklessly when he crashed?

c. Describing times and events—"frequency" adverbs

In section b, we discussed -*ly* adverbs, which describe the way that the action is done. The adverbs in this section are *frequency adverbs*—they describe *how often* we do (or don't do) something.

These are the most common frequency adverbs, in order from the most to the least frequent:

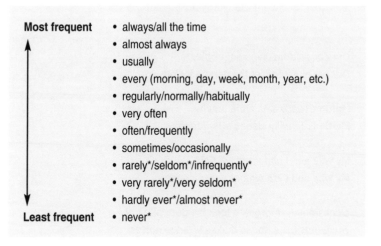

Most frequent
- always/all the time
- almost always
- usually
- every (morning, day, week, month, year, etc.)
- regularly/normally/habitually
- very often
- often/frequently
- sometimes/occasionally
- rarely*/seldom*/infrequently*
- very rarely*/very seldom*
- hardly ever*/almost never*

Least frequent
- never*

Note: * These frequency adverbs describe "negative" situations (infrequently = *not* frequently; never = *not* ever). When we use them in a sentence, they already imply a negative, so the verb is always in the affirmative, not the negative.

| correct: | **We *never* go to the movies nowadays.** |
| incorrect: | **We *never* don't go to the movies nowadays.** |

| correct: | **Monique *seldom* speaks French at home.** |
| incorrect: | **Monique *seldom* doesn't speak French at home.** |

Because frequency adverbs describe repeated actions or habits, they are almost never used with progressive tenses: mostly, they are used with simple or perfect tenses.

Frequency adverbs can be used in several places in a sentence. They usually come just ahead of the main verb. If a sentence is long or complex, frequency adverbs can also follow *be*. Occasionally, we use some frequency adverbs (but *not* all of them) to introduce the sentence by putting them first, at the very beginning. If we use them that way, we put a comma (,) after them. When we do this, we are emphasizing that adverb, just as if we underlined it in writing.

Our car *seldom* gives us problems.
Our car is *seldom* at the garage for repairs.

Martin *usually* eats a big lunch.
Martin is *usually* sleepy after lunch.

My wife and I *almost never* fight.
My wife and I are *almost never* alone.

***Occasionally*, I forget to lock the door at night.**
***Sometimes*, the house makes strange noises.**
***Usually*, John goes jogging in the morning, but sometimes, he jogs at night.**

Time Prepositions

In English, we make a big distinction between a short action or event that lasts only a brief time and a continuing action over a longer time. Simple and progressive tenses (see Chapter 2, section a, *Verbs—all about time*) illustrate this idea clearly, but it isn't limited to that. We use several words to show that we are talking about either a point in time or a length of time. Some of these words are used only with past, present, or future situations; others are used with two or all three situations.

Words used for points in time

- at

used with clock times, *some* times of day, and most holidays—for past, present, or future

> I'll meet you for dinner *at* 7:30.
>
> The board of directors met *at* 10:00, then had a lunch break *at* noon.
>
> My plane arrived *at* 11:53.
>
> It's hard to sleep *at* night.
>
> The kids always want to watch a TV show just *at* dinnertime.
>
> Are you usually away *at* Christmas and New Year's?
>
> Paul will be going home *at* Thanksgiving, but not *at* Easter.

With the general name of the holiday, we usually use *at* (or sometimes *for*), but if we talk about a specific time during the holiday, we use *on*, not *at*.

> We'll be here *on* Christmas Eve, but we're going to Jim's house *on* Christmas Day.

THE BASICS

- on

used with dates, days, and most holidays—for past, present, or future

---

Let's meet *on* the 16th.

Was Bill and Kim's anniversary *on* May 4th?

Tim works out at the gym *on* Mondays and Wednesdays, and he jogs *on* Tuesdays and Fridays.

We're planning a big party *on* New Year's Eve.

On Mondays is not the same as *on Monday*. If we do something regularly on a certain day each week, we add *-s* to the name of the day.

I teach oil painting on *Fridays*. (= every Friday; used with simple present)

I'm teaching oil painting on *Friday*. (= only this coming Friday; used with present progressive)

- in

used in two separate ways, for points in time and lengths of time, with specific years, months, seasons, and *some* times of day to show specific points in time—for past, present, or future

---

Will the world really be different *in* (the year) 2050?

Man first walked on the moon *in* 1969.

This chest was made *in* the 18th century.

Margaret is going to take her vacation *in* September.

Do you like to travel *in* summer?

Granddad usually rests *in* the afternoon.

I'm always hungrier at night than *in* the morning.

Words used for lengths of time

- by

used with clock times, times of day, specific weeks, months, years, and most holidays to show the length of time an action continues from one point in time up to another point *and then stops*—for past, present, or future; can be either simple or perfect tenses, depending on the action; slightly different from *until* because *by* means before this point or earlier, but *not* later whereas *until* simply means *up to* and sounds less urgent; also used with past perfect tense in the phrase *by the time*

Louis should graduate *by* June. (no later than June)

Can I get to the airport *by* 4:00? (4:00 or earlier, but not later)

The package will arrive *by the end of* next week. (next Friday or before)

I'll need those reports *by* Thursday at the latest.

Everyone had started dessert *by the time* George arrived.

My parents had been married five years *by the time* I was born.

Ted will have saved enough for a new car by *Christmas*.

- until

used with clock times, times of day, specific weeks, months, years, and most holidays to show the length of time from one point in time up to another point—for past, present, or future; very close to *by* (see above) in meaning, but less emphatic

Howard didn't drive *until* he was 25.

***Until* when do you serve dinner?**

They'll be remodeling this place *until* the middle of April.

I can't wait *until* tomorrow!

The shipment won't arrive *until* the end of next week.

THE BASICS

- since

used with clock times, dates, days, weeks, months, years, and holidays to talk about an action that began at a specific time in the past and continues to the present; mostly used with perfect tenses—especially the present perfect (see Chapter 7, section a, *Other verb tenses—the perfect tenses*)

We've owned this house *since* 1958. (and still own it)

The washing machine hasn't worked *since* last Tuesday. (and still doesn't work)

Ellen hasn't cut her hair *since* she was 11.

You haven't paid us *since* the 20th of August.

I haven't used the oven *since* Thanksgiving.

***Since* when have you been eating meat?**

Martin has worked late every night *since* his promotion.

- for

used with number of minutes, hours, days, weeks, months, or years to show the length of time an action lasts—for past, present, or future; often uses perfect tenses; unlike *since*, the length of time is important, not the starting point

Scott can't go without a cigarette *for* five minutes.

We waited at the airport *for* three hours.

Don and Anita will stay in Rome *for* only two days.

Dad worked for the same company *for* 25 years.

Harry has had money problems *for* a long time.

Eva expected to be married *for* life, but she and Sam were together *for* only three years.

- in (with future time)

the second way we use *in* is with lengths of time to show the distance from "now" into the future; sometimes also to talk about the distance into the future from a past point in time

I'll be there *in* five minutes to pick you up.

Mark expects to become a vice-president *in* a few years.

Laura made her first million *in* less than five years.

Terry drives so well, we got to the office *in* 30 minutes—half the usual time.

Willy and Jean expect to move *in* two or three years.

My boss said he'd be back *in* an hour.

- ago

  used with lengths of time to show distance from "now" back to past events—only for past tenses; *ago* always comes after lengths of time

We first met 15 years *ago*.

How long *ago* did you come to this country?

There was a terrible fire here a few years *ago*.

Up until a few days *ago*, Linda was very healthy.

I arrived two days *ago*, but my luggage got here only yesterday.

Ted bought his computer just a week *ago*, but it's already broken.

To talk about the distance from one past event to another, farther back, we use . . . *earlier* or . . . *before* (*that*), not *ago*. It's slightly more formal or businesslike to use . . . *earlier*.

speaking "now": **I last saw him three days *ago*.**

speaking "then": **The accident was last Monday, and I saw him three days *before* (*that*).**

speaking "then": **The accident was last Monday, and I saw him three days *earlier*.**

Other time expressions

Other time expressions are markers—we use them together with certain tenses.

For present (but not necessarily *immediate* present) events

now

this . . .   (*morning, afternoon, evening, week, month, season, year*, etc.)

at the moment

today

tonight   (if "now" is afternoon or evening)

every   (*minute, hour, day, morning, afternoon, evening, week, month, year*, etc.)

from . . . to . . .

between . . . and . . .

so far

until now

up to now

up to this point   (used with present perfect tense)

For past events

then

last time

last . . .   (*evening, week, month, season, year*, etc.)

yesterday   (*morning, afternoon, evening, night*)

recently

later   (from one past event into the future)

at that time

after that

that . . .   (*day, week, month, season, year*, etc.)

from . . . to . . .

between . . . and . . .

until then

up to that point   (used with past perfect tense)

For future events

next time	
next	(*week, month, season, year,* etc.)
tomorrow	
from now	
tonight	(if "now" is morning)
this coming . . .	(*week, month, season, year,* etc.)
the upcoming	(+ noun)
from . . . to . . .	
between . . . and . . .	
until that time	(used with simple future tense)
from this point on	(used with simple future tense)

Talking About Quantities

a. Some/any/no/none

When an English speaker wants to talk about a specific or definite quantity of nouns, the speaker will use *there is a . . .* , or *there are (three) . . . s* (see Chapter 3, section g, *There is/there are*). If the speaker wants to talk about the amount of the noun(s) in an approximate or general way, he or she will use *some/any/no/none*.

* some

used for *affirmatives*—either as a "yes" answer to a question or as a statement; also used for questions *if* there is a reason to think the answer probably will be *yes*

There are *some* blankets in the closet.

Shall I make *some* coffee for you?

I'd like *some* lunch, please.

There are *some* water spots on the ceiling.

Bobby found *some* old records in the attic. Let's listen to *some* (of them) after dinner.

Could we have *some* bread with our food, please?

Dad needs *some* more medicine.

Do you need *some* help? (listener seems to need help)

---

* any

used for *negatives*—either as a negative answer to a question or as a statement; also used for questions if the speaker has no idea at all whether the answer will be *yes* or *no*

Do you have *any* small bills on you? I don't have *any* ones or fives with me. (ones or fives = $1 or $5 bills)

There isn't *any* bread left, and I forgot to get *some* at the store.

It seems that Andrew doesn't have *any* friends, but maybe he has *some* we don't know about.

I can't talk—I don't have *any* time now.

Are there *any* files on the Norris case?

Harold says there aren't *any* good programs on TV, but I think there are *some*.

Did Stella's parents leave a will or *any* other document when they died?

I can't find *any* of my winter coats—where are they?

Did Sarah meet *any* nice or interesting people on her cruise to Alaska?

- no

  close to *not any* in meaning; used instead of *not any* when we want to emphasize or strengthen a *negative* statement—either as a *negative* answer to a question or as a statement; because it is so emphatic, we use it very carefully in answers—especially when answering a request; seldom used for questions, and never used without a noun, unlike *none*

Sam has absolutely *no* ability to budget his money. (not any)

There's *no* gas in the car!

Do you have *any* idea where the kids are? I've *no* idea at all. (no idea = don't know)

Finish your homework, Larry, or there will be *no* TV after dinner.

Conrad and Pam have *no* time for breakfast during the week.

The doctor says I can eat *some* eggs occasionally, but absolutely *no* bacon.

Why are there *no* reports from the West Coast branches?*

Your daughter has *no* common sense!

We have *no* reason to criticize our salespeople, just the product.

THE BASICS

Note: * The speaker could also have said *Why aren't there <u>any</u> reports* . . ., but using *no* shows either that he or she is displeased or that the reports are badly needed.

- none

used—always *without* a noun—for negatives—either as a negative answer to a question or as a statement; the speaker and listener must first agree on what *none* stands for since the noun isn't usually used in the same sentence; seldom used for actual questions, but the speaker may use it to confirm the other person's negative statement (*Are you sure there are <u>none</u>?*); often used for emphasis after a statement with *not any*

I've checked on the tickets, but there are *none* left.

Margaret told me (that) *none* of Tom's business associates came to the hospital.

Is there *any* shampoo in the closet? There's *none* in the shower.

None out here, either.

Ted and Mandy's money all goes for the rent—and there's *none* left for luxuries.

Fred's so busy he has *no* time for his family and *none* for a social life, either.

We asked our neighbor to lend us a hammer and *some* nails, but he had *none*.

If the speaker and listener agree on the subject, the noun can be left out with *some, any,* and *none*, but not with *no*.

Would you like *some* <u>wine</u>? →→→ Yes, I'd like *some*.

Would you like *some* <u>wine</u>? →→→ No, thanks, I don't want *any*.

I'd like to offer you *some* <u>wine</u>, but there's *none* left.

With *some* and *any*, we can use these questions and short-form answers:

Do you have *some/any* . . . ?	→→→	**Yes, I do./** **No, I don't.**** (OR **Yes, I have./** **No, I haven't.**)
Is there *some/any* . . . ?	→→→	**Yes, there is./** **No, there isn't.** (OR **No, there's *none*.**)
Are there *some/any* . . . ?	→→→	**Yes, there are./** **No, there aren't.** (OR **No, there are *none*.**)

Note: **In addition to *have*, other verbs often used with *some* or *any* include *want, know, need, would like, buy,* and *get*.

Since *no* and *none* replace *not*, it's incorrect to use *not* in the same sentence.

correct:	**We don't have *any* hot water.**
correct:	**We have no hot *water*.**
incorrect:	**We don't have no hot water.**

If we want to add a stronger negative emphasis to *any, not any, no,* or *none* (but <u>not</u> to *some* because it sounds positive instead of negative), we can do it by using the phrase *at all* after the noun.

Do you have *any time* *at all* this week?	→→→	**Sorry, *none at all*.**
Is there *no* hope *at all* for my father, doctor?	→→→	**Unfortunately, there's *no* hope *at all*.**

THE BASICS

We use these same concepts to combine *some/any/no* with certain nouns to create new words (*compounds*). They follow most of the same rules and are very useful for general descriptions, statements, or questions. They are always used in a singular form.

• someone, anyone, no one

used for people in general situations, such as talking to—or asking a question of—a group of people without concentrating on a specific person

Does *anyone* know the name of this wine?

Could *someone* help me carry this to the car?
(one of the group of listeners)

Harry, I hear *someone* moving around downstairs.

Is *anyone* there?

There's *no one* there, Ann—it's just the cat.

Sue didn't think *anyone* in the office knew about her car accident.

Why does *no one* protest this kind of injustice?

• something, anything, nothing

used the same way for talking about objects, animals, or even situations

There's *something* burning—check the oven.

Is there *anything* you would like to discuss with me?

I haven't found *anything* to give Barbara for her birthday yet.

Make sure you wear *something* warm—it's going to snow.

Chris couldn't say *anything* when he got the news.

Helena won't allow *anything* red in her garden.

***Nothing*? Not even red roses?**

There's *nothing* in the fridge—let's order a pizza!
(fridge = refrigerator)

The police questioned the suspect for 10 hours, but he told them *nothing*.

• somewhere, anywhere, nowhere

used the same way for talking about places

Kelly left her keys *somewhere*, but she wasn't sure where.

I can't find my other glove *anywhere*.

We'd like to go *somewhere* casual for dinner.

I'm never going *anywhere* with Roger again—he's so boring!

There's *somewhere* I'd like to take you that I know you would enjoy.

Right now, there's *nowhere* I want to be except in bed.

Donald's life has no direction—it's going *nowhere*.

Alternative forms are:

---

someone, anyone, no one →→→ somebody, anybody, nobody

somewhere, anywhere, nowhere →→→ someplace, anyplace, no place

---

We spell some of the compounds of *no* with two words (*no one, no place*), but others are only one word (*nothing, nobody*), so be careful when writing them.

b. Much/many; little/few

There are two basic kinds of nouns in English: nouns you can count (*one book, two books,* etc.) and nouns you can't count (*wine, money, power, happiness*). When we talk about general quantities, and the quantity is large, we use the word *much* for *noncountable* nouns (nouns that already represent quantity and don't have any real plural form) or *many* for *countable* nouns (nouns we can add an *-s* or other plural ending to). Understanding this difference is very important because many other kinds of communication in English are based on this idea.

Much (for noncountable nouns)

advice	
air	
anger	He showed much anger during the trial.
beauty	
bread	How much bread do we need?
cattle	(cows, etc.)
chicken*	(= meat of chicken)
cloth	(= material, fabric)
clothing/clothes	
coffee	
crime	(= statistic; scale)
damage	The hurricane caused much damage.
dirt	
film	(= for cameras; the art of cinema)
fish*	
food	
fruit	(= *different kinds* of fruit)
fur	(= "material")
furniture	
garbage	
gasoline	How much gasoline should I put in the tank?
glass	(= material for windows, etc.)
gold	
grammar	
grass	
hair	(= all the hair—usually on the head; hairs = one or two strands of hair)
happiness	
health	
homework	I have too much homework.
ice	
information	
jewelry	

knowledge	
light	(= sunlight, daylight, moonlight, etc.)
lighting	(= artificial light)
literature	
luggage/baggage	
machinery	
mail	
meat	
merchandise	
milk	
money	There's no such thing as too much money.
music	
news	
noise*	
oil	
pain	He's in so much pain.
paper	(= blank paper)
peace	
postage	
poultry	(= chickens, etc.)
sand	
science	
silver	
soda	How much soda will we need for the party?
soil	
sound	
time	
traffic	There's so much traffic.
trouble*	
vocabulary	
water	
wealth	
wine	
wool	

Many (for countable nouns)

bills	How many bills do we have to pay this week?
birds	
books	
cars	There are so many cars on the road.
chairs	
chickens	(= living)
cookies	How many cookies did Bobby eat before dinner?
crimes	(= individual cases)
envelopes	
films	(= movies)
fishes	(= different kinds of fish)
flowers	There are so many kinds of flowers.
fruits	(= different kinds of fruit)
furs	(= fur coats, etc.)
glasses	(= wine glasses, water glasses, etc.)
goods	(= merchandise; possessions)
ice cubes	
lamps	
lawns	
letters	
lights	(= wall lights, ceiling lights, outdoor lights)
noises*	
papers	(= documents, letters, etc.)
pens	
people	There are so many people in the world.
seats	
(sheets of) **paper**	(= blank paper)
soft drinks	
songs	
stamps	

steaks	How many steaks are in the freezer?
suitcases	
times	(= moments; occasions)
trees	

Note: *Many words have both countable and noncountable forms, but they have different meanings.

chicken = chicken meat for food	**chickens = live chickens**
fish = fish as something to eat	**fishes = many species (usually *alive*)**
glass = material for windows, etc.	**glasses = for drinking; for eyesight**
sports = the category of sports	**(a) sport/sports = various sports**
noise = unpleasant sound level	**noises = specific sounds**
paper = blank sheets of paper	**papers = documents or letters**
trouble = a difficult situation	**troubles = various problems**

Even noncountable nouns can be counted if we use certain words, followed by *of*.

much liquor	many *bottles of* **liquor**
much work	many *hours of* **work**
much water	many *glasses of* **water**
much paper	many *sheets of* **paper**
much disease	many *cases of* **disease**
much clothing	many *items of* **clothing**

THE BASICS

In sentences, we use *much/many* most often with *there is/there are*, but we can use different verbs as well.

There are *many people* in the park today.

There isn't *much time* before the concert.

Why are there so *many dogs* outside that house?

I never saw *much snow* in Rome.

How *much wine* do they produce in Australia?

Have there been *many accidents* at this intersection?

How *many operations* has Aunt Ellen had?

They don't use *much coal* for heating in the United States.

Lily has *many cats*.

We don't eat *much beef*, but we eat *many vegetables*.

That author has written *many books*, but he doesn't write *much* nowadays.

We can also use *much/many* without any noun if the listener and speaker have already decided what the noun is.

Is there some more cake in the kitchen?	→→→	There isn't *much* left.
Does Danny have any brothers and sisters?	→→→	Yes, he has *many*.

In casual speech, most English speakers use the phrase *a lot of* instead of *much* or *many*. With *a lot of*, it doesn't matter whether you are talking about noncountable nouns or countable nouns. We do use *much* or *many* if we want to emphasize the quantity of a noun or if we are disagreeing with someone's opinion.

Tony watches *many* sports programs.	→→→	Tony watches *a lot of* sports programs.
I don't spend *a lot of* money on clothes.	→→→	I don't spend *much* money on clothes.

Most English speakers add small words for *emphasis* (called *intensifiers*) when using *much* or *many*. The most popular ones are *very*, *so*, and *too*. They come just before the word *much* or *many*. If we use *a lot of*, we never put any intensifier in the sentence.

Is there *very much* snow in Vermont?

Philip has *so many* neckties.

This coat costs *too much* (money).

We identify large quantities with *much* and *many*. When we want to talk about small quantities in a general way, we use the opposites of *much* and *many*—*little* for noncountable nouns, and *few* for countable nouns. Even though the answer will be *little* or *few*, the question is always *how much* or *how many*.

Ben doesn't have much money.	→→→	Ben has *little* money.
I don't see many films.	→→→	I see *few* films.
There isn't much traffic on Sunday mornings.	→→→	There's *little* traffic on Sunday mornings.
There don't seem to be many serious books now.	→→→	There seem to be *few* serious books now.

Schoolchildren don't eat much fruit.	→→→	Schoolchildren eat *little* fruit.
How much gas does your car use?	→→→	It uses very *little* (gas).
How many speeding tickets have you gotten?	→→→	I've gotten *few* (tickets).

c. Little/a little; few/a few

A small word like *a* can make a big difference in meaning. The difference between *little* and *a little* or *few* and *a few* is significant. We use the words *little* and *few* to talk about quantities that are small, not large. When we say *a* little or *a* few, however, we are (quite emphatically) saying that at least a quantity, even though it is small, does exist.

Did Alice eat *many* cookies?	→→→	No, she ate *few*.
		(= not many)
Did Alice eat *any* cookies?	→→→	Yes, she ate *a* few.
		(= a small amount, but not many)
Is there *much* snow in April?	→→→	No, there's very *little*.
		(= not much)
Is there *any* snow in April?	→→→	Sometimes there's *a* little.
		(= a small amount, but not much)

We use the intensifiers *very, so,* and *too* with *little* and *few*, but not with *a little* and *a few*. Instead, we use *just* or *only*. Another difference is that we can use *a little* and *a few* to mean "extra" or "additional" if we add the word *more* to the sentence.

Bob, have a *little more* meatloaf. (= extra amount)

If Bonnie and Kevin work *a few more* years, they'll be able to retire.

Mother has aged *a little more* since Christmas.
(= additional signs of age)

If I lose *only a few more* pounds, I'll be able to wear my nice clothes again. (= extra weight loss)

With *just a little more* effort, Jim could be a professional skier. (= additional training)

Grandpa is 73, but he still has a *few* "lady friends." (= not many, but some)

B
THE DETAILS

7 | Other Verb Tenses

a. The perfect tenses

The four major tenses in English are the simple present, simple past, simple future, and present perfect. There are six perfect tenses: the present, past, and future perfect, and three progressive forms (also called the *–ing form*). Perfect tenses are important because they show a finished ("perfect") action within a larger time frame—the present, past, or future.

We form all perfect tenses with the helping verb *have* and the past participle of the main verb. For the future perfect tense, we also need the helping verb *will*. Pay attention to the word order in the questions.

- present perfect

affirmative:	I *have* eaten.
	He *has* eaten.
affirmative (short answer):	Yes, I *have*.
	Yes, he *has*.
negative:	I *haven't* eaten.
	He *hasn't* eaten.
negative (short answer):	No, I *haven't*.
	No, he *hasn't*.
questions:	*Have* you eaten?
	Has he eaten?
	What *have* you *done*?
	What *has* he *done*?

- past perfect

affirmative:	I *had* eaten.
	He *had* eaten.
affirmative (short answer):	Yes, I *had*.
	Yes, he *had*.
negative:	I *hadn't* eaten.
	He *hadn't* eaten.
negative (short answer):	No, I *hadn't*.
	No, he *hadn't*.
questions:	*Had* you eaten?
	Had he eaten?
	What *had* you *done*?
	What *had* he *done*?

- future perfect

affirmative:	I *will have* eaten.
	He *will have* eaten.
affirmative (short answer):	Yes, I *will*.
	Yes, I *will have*.
	Yes, he *will have*.
negative:	I *won't have* eaten.
	He *won't have* eaten.
negative (short answer):	No, I *won't*.
	No, I *won't have*.
	No, he *won't have*.
questions:	*Will* you *have* eaten?
	Will he *have* eaten?
	What *will* you *have* done?
	What *will* he *have* done?

THE DETAILS

We form all perfect *progressive* tenses with the helping verbs *have* and *be*, and the *present* participle (*eat* → *eating*, *drive* → *driving*, *win* → *winning*) of the main verb. For the future perfect tense, we also need the helping verb *will*. Most of the rules about progressive tenses apply to perfect progressive tenses as well (see Chapter 2, section e, *Simple and progressive verb forms*).

- present perfect progressive

affirmative:	I *have been* eat*ing*.
	He *has been* eat*ing*.
affirmative (short answer):	Yes, I *have*.
	Yes, I *have been*.
	Yes, he *has been*.
negative:	I *haven't been* eat*ing*.
	He *hasn't been* eat*ing*.
negative (short answer):	No, I *haven't*.
	No, I *haven't been*.
	No, he *hasn't been*.
questions:	*Have* you *been* eat*ing*?
	Has he *been* eat*ing*?
	What *have* you *been* do*ing*?
	What *has* he *been* do*ing*?

- past perfect progressive

affirmative:	I *had been* eat*ing*.
	He *had been* eat*ing*.
affirmative (short answer):	Yes, I *had been*.
	Yes, he *had been*.
negative:	I *hadn't been* eat*ing*.
	He *hadn't been* eat*ing*.
negative (short answer):	No, I *hadn't been*.
	No, he *hadn't been*.

questions:	_Had_ you _been_ eat_ing_?
	Had he _been_ eat_ing_?
	What _had_ you _been_ eat_ing_?
	What _had_ he _been_ eat_ing_?

* future perfect progressive

affirmative:	I _will have been_ eat_ing_.
	He _will have been_ eat_ing_.
affirmative (short answer):	Yes, I _will have been_.
	Yes, he _will have been_.
negative:	I _won't have been_ eat_ing_.
	He _won't have been_ eat_ing_.
negative (short answer):	No, I _won't have been_.
	No, he _won't have been_.
questions:	_Will_ you _have been_ eat_ing_?
	Will he _have been_ eat_ing_?
	What _will_ you _have been_ eat_ing_?
	What _will_ he _have been_ eat_ing_?

As you know, there are regular and irregular verbs (see Chapter 2). The past participle of all _regular_ verbs is identical to the simple past tense, which always ends in _−ed_. Irregular verbs often also have past participles that are the same as their simple past forms, but many have a different form for the past participle. Dictionaries usually give only the simple form (_talk, drink, be_) for regular verbs, but also give the past tense and the past participle for irregular verbs (_speak → spoke → spoken; take → took → taken; be → was/were → been_). Check the dictionary if you are unsure of a particular verb's past participle.

REGULAR VERBS

| simple form | simple past | past participle |
| ask | asked | asked |

THE DETAILS

call	called	called
stop	stopped	stopped
talk	talked	talked

IRREGULAR VERBS

simple form	simple past	past participle
be	was	been
bring	brought	brought
do	did	done
drink	drank	drunk
drive	drove	driven
eat	ate	eaten
fall	fell	fallen
have	had	had
keep	kept	kept
make	made	made
put	put	put
show	showed	shown
sleep	slept	slept

So, if you know the past participle of a verb, it's easy to form any of the perfect tenses.

present perfect	past perfect	future perfect
have/has been	*had* been	*will have* been
have/has brought	*had* brought	*will have* brought
have/has done	*had* done	*will have* done
have/has drunk	*had* drunk	*will have* drunk
have/has driven	*had* driven	*will have* driven
have/has eaten	*had* eaten	*will have* eaten

But when do you use a simple tense and when do you use a perfect tense? A simple tense tells the listener only if the action is present, past, or future—a single point in time. A perfect tense puts that action in a time frame. Although the action may be finished, the time frame you are talking about continues beyond the action.

Each perfect tense is different and has its own uses, so let's look at each one separately.

Present perfect

Present perfect is used to connect something that started in the past, but continues in the present. You need the present perfect, not the simple past, if you can use either of the time words *since* or *for* in the sentence, or if the sentence answers the question *How long.* . . . If you can use the time words *in* or *on* in the sentence, or if the sentence answers the question *How long ago* . . . , you need the simple past.

Beth and John *have been married for* 21 years.
(and still are married) →→→ **They *were married in* 1978.**

James Addams *has been* our doctor *since* 1990. (and still is)
→→→ **He *became* our doctor *in* 1990.**

***How long has* Ed *been* in the hospital?** →→→ **He *'s been* there *since* last Tuesday.** (and he's there now while we are speaking)

We use the present perfect to talk about these situations:

- something that began in the past, but has continued into the present (or that has some connection with the present); usually used with the time words *for* or *since*

The Barrs *have lived* here *for* 18 years. (and they still live here now)

Mother *has used* Chanel No. 5 *since* her wedding in 1957.
(she used it then and she continues to use it now)

Joe *has driven* a BMW *for* 10 years.
(he drove it 10 years ago and he still drives it "today")

Marsha *has thought* a lot about moving to a smaller home *since* her children married. (she is still thinking about it now)

THE DETAILS

- an action that is finished, but that happened during a time frame that isn't finished yet; usually used with the time word *already*

Has Mark *already spoken* with you about the position in London? (the discussion is finished, but the position in London is still open, or the time frame of the discussion— "today," "this week," etc.—isn't finished yet)

Mr. and Mrs. Douglas *have already left* for the airport. (they are en route, but neither their flight nor "today" is finished)

The boys *have already eaten* their breakfast. (their breakfast is finished, but "today," "this morning" is still continuing)

I*'ve already read* today's paper—I read it on the train. (reading is finished, but "today" is still continuing; both the reading and the train trip are finished, so the simple past is used instead)

- something that we (or a third person) have or haven't experienced in our lifetimes; the event is over, but the lifetime continues; always used with *ever* (for questions only, *not* affirmative statements or answers) or *never* (for negative statements or answers)*

Has Carrie *ever been to* Disneyland?
Tom *has never eaten* sushi.
Has Paul *ever tried* to discuss his problems with someone?
Ron and I *have never had* an argument about money.
Susan *has never come* home this late before.

Note: *Using *ever* or *never*. We use *ever* only for questions, not when we give an affirmative answer to an "*ever*" question. If we use *never*, it already supplies the negative, so it's incorrect to use *not* in the same sentence.

question:	**Have you *ever* been to London?**
affirmative answer:	**Yes, I *have* been to London.**

negative answer:	**No, I've *never* been to London.**
negative statement:	**I've *never* been to London.**
<u>incorrect:</u>	**(Yes,) I *have ever* been to London.**
<u>incorrect:</u>	**I *haven't never* been to London.**

- something physical—usually an illness or symptoms that began in the past, but that the subject hasn't "recovered from" yet; the time words *since*, *for*, and *not yet*** are used

Barbara *has felt* ill *since* her pregnancy began last month.
(she is still pregnant)

Mary *has had* high blood pressure for the last five years or so.
(and she still has it)

All of us *have caught* the flu. (they aren't well yet)

Lola's father *has suffered* from insomnia for several years.
(and he still does)

Note: **See section b, for details about these time words.

Some native speakers use the simple past when they should really use the present perfect tense. That happens when they mentally focus on the time the action finished instead of the larger time frame (today, this week, this month, this year, in . . . 's lifetime, etc.).

correct:	**I've read the paper today./I've already read the paper.** (because "today" is not finished)
correct:	**I read the paper this morning.** (because "this morning" is finished)
<u>incorrect:</u>	**I read the paper today.** (incorrect because "today" isn't finished; the speaker really means *earlier* today or "this morning"; because those earlier time frames are past, he or she may tend to use the simple past)

THE DETAILS

Using the present perfect instead of the simple past definitely changes the meaning of even a basic statement.

I'*ve* (already) *had* two cups of coffee today. (he or she may still have more coffee "today")

I *had* two cups of coffee today. (he or she probably doesn't plan to have coffee again "today")

As a guideline for choosing between a perfect tense and a simple tense, ask yourself whether *the larger time frame* is completely (not just partially) finished (if yes, use a simple tense) or if the time frame is continuing beyond the action described (if yes, use a perfect tense).

To help identify the difference, the following words indicate a *continuing or unfinished* time frame for which you need a perfect tense: *up to now* (only for present perfect), *up until then, so far, by, by the time* (only for past perfect), *today, this week/month/year, already, still, not . . . yet, until, during, since, for, how long.*

For is used with the simple past and also with the past and present perfect tenses. *How long* can also be used with the simple past, but if the situation that *how long* asks about has continued up to "now," you would use the present perfect.

These words are used to identify a *point in time* or a past time frame, so you need a simple tense: *ago, at, on, in* (+ year), *yesterday, last week/month/year, then, at that time, when* (question word).

One more thing to remember about the present perfect is the difference between *have/has been* and *have/has gone*. When we use *have been* (only if followed by the prepositions *to* or *at*), we mean that the subject went to or was at a place during an unfinished time frame, but *is no longer at that place*. When we use *have gone* (meaning *go to/go into a place*), we mean that the subject went there earlier and *is still there* "now." This is also true when talking about sports or activities with the verb *go*, such as *go skiing, go hiking, go for a walk*. This rule doesn't cover idiomatic or adjective/verb phrases using *be* or *go* (*be tired, go through*, etc.).

The Williams family *has gone* to Mexico.
(and they are still there "now")
The Williams family *has been* to Mexico.
(and they have just come back)
Roy *has gone* (out) bowling tonight—he'll be back by 10:30.
Roy *has been* (out) bowling tonight—he's just *come home* now.

Present perfect progressive

Present perfect progressive is used when a situation or action began in the past, continued into the present, *and is still continuing "now"*; it answers the question *How long . . . been –ing*; usually used with the time words *for* or *since*.

I *haven't been exercising since* I caught this cold.
(still not recovered; still not exercising)

Mary and Howard *have been dating for* the last three years.
(they are still dating)

Andrew *has been paying off* his student loans *for* three years.
(he hasn't finished paying yet; *pay off* = pay part of a debt each week/month)

I*'ve been cooking* this Thanksgiving dinner *for* four days.
(the cooking isn't finished yet)

Erica *has been working on* her monthly report all morning.
(she's still working on it)

The present perfect progressive is different from both the present perfect and the present progressive. The action or situation the present perfect describes is finished, even if the larger time frame is not; the present progressive describes an action happening "now," with no hint of when the action started. The present perfect progressive tells us that the action started in the past and is still continuing.

present progressive: **Bob *is reading* the newspaper *now*.**
(we don't know *when* he started reading it)

THE DETAILS

present perfect:	**Bob _has read_ the newspaper.** (we know only that he _finished_ reading it _within an unfinished time frame_— today, this week, recently, during his lifetime, etc.)
present perfect progressive:	**Bob _has been reading_ the newspaper _for_ an hour.** (we now know that he _started reading_ the paper _an hour ago_, and he is _still reading_ it at this moment)

The future perfect progressive and past perfect progressive tenses both show continuing actions that go either from "now" into the future (_future_ perfect progressive) or from one past point to another past point closer to "now" (_past_ perfect progressive). Otherwise, they follow the same rules as the present perfect progressive.

Past perfect

Past perfect is used about a situation or action that began in the past and continued forward, toward _but not up to the present_. It usually describes two actions or situations, _both in the past_: a _completed_ action that started at one point in the past and ended before another, slightly later, past action. The second action or situation is usually in the simple past tense. The past perfect answers the questions _By what time had . . ._ or _Until when/what time had. . . ._ It is usually used with the time words _until_, _by_, or _by the time_ (_by the time_ is followed by the action in the simple past). Occasionally, _by the time_ can be replaced with _when_, _after_, or _before_.

By the time Susan and Joe _had decided_ to start a family, they were over 40.

Bill _had washed_ all the dishes and (_had_) _cleaned_ the house _by the time_ I got home from class.

By the time Terry _had finished_ his first year with the company, he was already looking for his next job.

Sally's hair _had turned_ completely gray _by_ her 25th birthday. (_turned_ = became/changed into)

Just *after* Ken *had bought* an expensive new house, his company went bankrupt.

Had Maurice already *seen* the latest sales figures *before* he made his speech?

We *hadn't fixed* the damage to our house *when* the second earthquake struck. (*struck = happened*—for disasters, serious illness, etc.)

We use the past perfect to describe the connection between two past actions or situations that happened one after the other.

By the time the doctors stopped the bleeding, the patient *had died* from shock.

When we got back from the party, Tony realized he *had forgotten* to lock the front door.

Sam *had already left* for school *before* the fire started.

Before I *had taken off* my coat, the kids started demanding a snack.

Future perfect

Future perfect is used about a situation or action that either began in the past or is starting "now," and is expected to continue until a specific future point in time, and then end. In addition to *have*, we almost always use the helping verb *will*, not *going to*, with the future perfect. The future perfect is usually used with the time words *by* or *by the time*; it is occasionally used with *when*. The simple present usually follows the time words.

Roy *will have completed* his 29th year with our company *by* this April.

By the time I'm 40, I *will have saved* $100,000.

This play is so boring—*by* the end of it, Dad *will have had* a two-hour nap. (nap = short sleep)

THE DETAILS

Chuck *will have broken* the heart of every girl in school *by the time* he graduates.

By what time do you think the mail *will have arrived*?

If our soccer team wins tonight's game, they *'ll have won* ten games in a row.

We *'ll have lived* here for five years *by* next Christmas.

We use the future perfect to describe a continuing action or situation that might start "now," or might have started earlier, but one we expect will be continuing until a future time.

It's very cold now, but I'm sure it *will have warmed up by* lunchtime.

By the time he graduates, Tony *will have spent* almost $100,000 on his education.

By the time the guests get here, Tina *will have polished* the table a dozen times.

Ron and Gina *will have been married* for 15 years *by* the end of this month.

I doubt whether the paint on the dining room walls *will have dried by* our Christmas party on the 20th.

b. More time words—already, still, not yet, not anymore

In addition to *since*, *for*, *by*, and *by the time*, the perfect tenses use several other time words that are very useful for showing if something has happened, is happening, or will or won't happen. They are:

• already

We use *already* to show that a situation or action has started by the point in time that we are talking about. *Already* is used only for questions or affirmative statements. For negative statements, we use *not yet*, and for questions with a slightly critical tone, we use *still*.

Gail had *already* been waiting for several hours when the repairman finally got there.

The train has *already* arrived, but Joyce *hasn't* gotten off *yet*.

- still

We use the word *still* when we mean that something is continuing, but that we expect it to end at some time. The opposite of *still* is *not anymore*, which tells us that an action or situation is not continuing. We use *still* in both affirmative and negative statements (*still hasn't/wasn't/isn't* . . .), as well as for questions.

Is Bobby *still* eating?

Joann *still* hasn't learned how to write.

George and Martha seemed unhappy together—I'm surprised that they're *still* married.

Our dog is 13, but he *still* likes to chase cars.

Henry is*n't* with that company *anymore*, but he *still* does consulting work for them.

My tenant *still* hasn't paid his rent.

- not yet

We use *not yet* when we mean that something has *not* happened up to the time we are talking about, but that either we expect it to happen soon or we know it did happen shortly after the time we are talking about (for past situations). It is used only for negative statements or answers; *yet* by itself is used for questions; for affirmative statements or answers, we use *already*.

The lecture *hasn't* started *yet*, but the speaker has *already* arrived.

Has Mr. Borden called *yet*? →→→→ No, *not yet*.

Louis has *already* put up the storm windows on the ground floor, but he *hasn't* done the upstairs *yet*.

> **Is Judy's blouse back from the dry cleaners** *yet?* →→→ *Not*
> *yet,* **but I'm expecting it today.**
>
> **Do we have to eat now? I'm** *not* **hungry** *yet.*

- not anymore

We use *not anymore* (or *not any longer*) to show that an action
or situation has ended. It's the opposite of *still*, which shows
that something is continuing.

> **Barbara doesn't work for us** *anymore,* **but she's** *still* **living in**
> **this city.**
>
> **Keith doesn't smoke** *anymore.*
>
> **Since I started my diet, I don't use milk in my coffee** *anymore,*
> **but I** *still* **put sugar in it.**
>
> **It's been two hours and Dora** *still* **hasn't called—I just don't**
> **want to wait for her** *anymore.*

c. Using modal auxiliaries—can, may, might, etc.

Modals are a form of helping verb (see Chapter 2, section c,
Helping verbs—auxiliaries), but in some ways they are quite
different from true helping verbs (such as *be, do,* and *have*).
We use helping verbs *only* as a way to form the different
tenses of other verbs. For example, the main meaning of *have*
is "to own" or "to possess." When we use *have* as a helping
verb to form the present perfect tense (*I have seen*), *have* is
meaningless except for its job to help form the present perfect.

Modals are different from true helping verbs because they each
have very specific meanings—often several different ones. The
purpose of modals is to show the feelings, reactions, attitudes,
or thoughts of the speaker about a situation or action (*I have
to wash this floor; Harry should visit his mother; Mom can
make better cookies than Aunt Sue; It will rain, it might even
snow;* etc.).

Modals and helping verbs are similar in these ways:

- Both modals and helping verbs must be used with a second
  verb (the *full verb*) to give the complete meaning of the sen-

tence; without the full verb, modals and helping verbs make no real sense.

- Both modals and helping verbs always come before, not after, the full verb.

- In sentences using modals and helping verbs, the full verb is usually in the simple form (*go, speak, write, take, eat,* etc.), although there are some exceptions. The modal or helping verb changes tense, *not* the full verb (*had to* go, *could* speak, *had been able to* write, etc.).

Tommy *couldn't finish* his homework because the computer broke.

The company *will have to start* to hire more women.

I'm *going to be able to buy* a new car next year.

Modals and helping verbs are different in these ways:

- Modals all have at least one meaning that shows the speaker's opinion of, or feelings about, a situation or action; helping verbs lose their real meanings completely, and act only as a mechanical way to form various English tenses.

- Most true modals have very few, if any, of the tenses full verbs have but many do have a general way of showing future or past situations; helping verbs, however, have all the tenses that full verbs have.

There are some other verbs that we use just like modals (because they are incomplete—and make no sense—without a second verb to complete their meaning), but that are not true modals because they have many of the different tenses that full verbs have. They are:

be able to

like to

need to

want to

Finally, there are two kinds of modals: those that are followed directly by the simple form of the full verb (Susie *can write*), and

THE DETAILS

those that are always followed by *to* before the verb (John *has to drive* two hours a day). These modals and modal-like verbs are always followed by *to* before the full verb:

have got to
have to
like to
need to
ought to
want to

Modal (present time)	Meaning(s)
be able to/not (isn't/aren't) able to; be unable to	almost the same as *can* (1)
can/can't	(1) ability; (2) possibility or potential; (3) asking for or giving permission (*casual* tone); (4) making requests (*casual* tone)
could/couldn't	(1) past form of *can*; (2) past ability; (3) asking permission or making requests; (4) unlikely possibility (*couldn't*); (5) possibility only in a certain situation (used with *if*)
had better/had better not	advice (stronger than either *should* or *ought to*)
have got to/haven't got to* have to/don't have to	same as, but stronger than, *have to* necessity (less urgent, more personal than *must*)
like to/don't (doesn't) like to	enjoyment (general, ongoing situations)
may/may not	(1) possible future situation; (2) asking or giving permission; (3) discuss possible explanations for behavior or situations

might/might not	(1) past forms of *may*; (2) doubtful future situation; (3) asking permission (*very* polite)—negative not used
must/don't (doesn't) have to (1)**	(1) necessity (stronger than *have to* or *have got to*);(2) strong probability
need to/don't (doesn't) need to	requirement (usually personal reasons)
ought to/ought not	(1) advice; (2) hinted responsibility or duty
should/shouldn't	(1) advice; (2) probability—no negative form; (3) logical belief
want to/don't (doesn't) want to	wishing; talking about preferences
will/won't	(1) definite future intent; (2) prediction; (3) making requests; (4) offering or inviting—negative form for (3) and (4) rarely used
would/wouldn't	(1) past form of *will;* (2) discussion of doubtful future event; (3) polite requests; part of phrases for asking permission

Note: *In British English, *have got to* is used for all situations that are expressed by *have to* and *have got to* in American English. For past situations, *had got to* is rarely used in American English; the negative, *hadn't got to* is used only in British English.

Note: **The negative form of *must* is *don't/doesn't have to* or *don't/doesn't need to*. We use *must not* only to forbid (strongly refuse permission) someone from doing something—especially with children.

Must I go to the party? →→→ Yes, *you must*. No, you *don't have to*. (No, you *don't need to*.)
You *mustn't* touch that. It's David's.
I *must* send in my tax form by April 15th. It *mustn't* be late.

To talk about necessity, in descending order of urgency, we use *must*, *have got to*, *have to*, and *need to*.

THE DETAILS

You *must* pay that traffic ticket this week.

(= the law)

I*'ve got to* put snow tires on the car today.

(= snow is likely)

Bill *has to* take his dog to the veterinarian on Thursday.

We *need to review* our stock portfolio, but first I *have to* do our budget.

(= budget is more urgent; changes in stock portfolio can wait for a short time)

George and Sandy really *need to* paint their front door.

(= it doesn't look good)

In present situations, *can* and *be able to* are very close in meaning, although *be able to* is more formal, and *can* just gives facts about ability; *be able to* sounds as if the subject has succeeded with effort.

Brendan *can* run five miles a day.

(= fact—maybe he has always been able to)

Brendan *is* (now/finally/at last) *able to* run five miles a day.

(= final result of effort)

I *can* buy a new house this year.

(= fact—maybe he or she could have bought one last year, too)

I *am able to* (now/finally/at last) buy a new house this year.

(= sounds as if he or she overcame problem or barrier— not enough savings, mortgage rates too high, etc.)

When we talk about past actions or situations with *could* and *was/were able to*, there is some difference in meaning. In the past tense, especially in affirmative statements, we use *was/were able to* for specific cases. We mostly use *could* for general statements. For most negative statements in the past tense, we tend to use *couldn't* for all situations, but we can also use *wasn't/weren't able to*.

Barbara *was able to* recover from her riding accident in 1977.
(specific case)

Doctors *could* repair minor damage to the spine even in 1977.
(general statement)

Barbara *couldn't* get over her fear of horses after the riding accident.

When we want to give advice to someone, there are several modals we use: *should*, *ought to*, and *had better*. Both *should* and *ought to* are equal in strength, but *ought to* has a slightly stronger message of "it's wrong if you don't," whereas *should* suggests "it's better if you do." *Had better* is quite different—especially if the speaker is giving advice to either the listener or another person, instead of talking about himself or herself. It suggests that something bad will happen if the subject doesn't follow that advice. It also has the strongest tone of criticism, so we are always very careful about using it.

I don't think you *should* park there.	(= it might be a traffic violation)
You *shouldn't* go to pastry shops with your friends if you are dieting.	(= dieting gets more difficult)
We *should* fill the car before leaving on our trip.	(= otherwise, we might run out of gas; fill the car = buy gasoline)
You *shouldn't* wash white and colored clothes together.	(= the colors might run together)
Sam *ought to* turn out the lights when he goes to bed.	(= it's expensive and wastes energy if he doesn't)
Tim *ought to* fix those steps.	(= somebody might fall)
You *had better* start saving money.	(= if not, you'll be poor when you retire)
Our neighbors *had better* stop having those noisy parties.	(= if they continue, I'll call the police)
You *had better not* use that tone of voice at the meeting.	(= if you do, you might lose your job)

THE DETAILS

Advice modals are a lot stronger in their negative forms than in their affirmative forms: *shouldn't* is quite a strong criticism, and *had better not* is almost a warning or threat. We seldom use *ought not* in American English except when we talk about a bad decision in the past (*The company <u>ought not to have fired</u> the sales manager*).

We use certain modals for making requests, others for asking permission, and some for both functions. Making requests and asking permission are *not* the same thing. Asking the listener if you (the speaker) or another person may do something is permission. Asking the listener or another person to do something *for you* is a request. Going from the most to least polite (but still definitely polite) request are these modals: *could, would, will, can*. We use *might* as a very polite way of asking permission, or for making requests about another person, *not* the listener.

Ways of Asking Permission	Ways of Making Requests
(from the most formal/polite to the most informal/casual)	
May I/he . . . ?	Could you/he . . . ?
Could I/he . . . ?	Would you please (do) . . . ?
Would you mind if I/he . . . ?	Would you mind (do*ing*) . . . ?
Would it be all right if I/he . . . ?	Will you (do this) . . . , please?
Can I/he . . . ?	Can you (help me/do this) . . . ?

Modal (past time)	Meaning(s)
was able to/wasn't (weren't) able to; was (were) unable to	not really the same as *could* (1)*
can/can't	no separate past form—see *could*
could/couldn't*; **could have/couldn't have**	(1) past form of *can*; (2) past ability; (3) no past form; (4) unlikely possibility (*couldn't have*); (5) no past form as modal
had better/had better not	no separate past form—see *should have*
had got to/no negative in past	same as, but stronger than *had to*

had to/didn't have to	necessity (less urgent, more personal than *must*)
liked to/didn't like to	enjoyment
(also: **used to like/ didn't use to like**)	earlier habit (negative is *use to*, not *used to*)
may have/may not have	no separate past form for (1) or (2)—see *might have*; (3) discussing possible explanations for past behavior/situations
might have/might not have	(1), (2), and (3)—no past form possible; (4) discussing possible but unlikely explanations for past behavior or situations (less likely than *may have*)
must have/must not have	(1) no past form—see *had to*; (2) discussing very probable explanations for past behavior situations
needed to/didn't need to	requirement (usually personal)
ought to have/ought not to have	discussing advisability or inadvisability of past actions, behavior, or decisions
should have/shouldn't have	(1) discussing advisability or inadvisability of past actions or behavior; (2) probability—no past form; (3) discussing logical outcome of past situation (often used when result was unexpected or shocking
wanted to/didn't want to	wishing; talking about past preferences
will/won't	no past forms—see *would have*
would have/wouldn't have	(1) past form of *will*; (2) talking about things that *didn't* happen

Note: *When we talk about a past situation using any modal that adds *have* for past time, we must use the full verb's past participle (*eaten, spoken, seen, been, gone*, etc.), not its dictionary form (*eat, speak, see, be, go*).

I *could have <u>danced</u>* all night.

Gina *might have <u>gone</u>* on vacation, but I think she *would have <u>called</u>* me first.

Larry *shouldn't have <u>parked</u>* in the crosswalk.

You *may have <u>broken</u>* your wrist when you fell.

Mary and Hal *were able to* get married after her divorce became final.

This *has to* be a mistake—Larry *couldn't have <u>stolen</u>* a car.

Mom *must have <u>gone</u>* out and *must not have <u>had</u>* time to write us a note.

We sometimes *needed to* borrow money from my parents when we were in college.

Perry and Anne *ought to have <u>invited</u>* us to their Christmas party.

Andy *should have <u>visited</u>* the dentist three months ago.

You *ought not to have <u>spoken</u>* so sharply to the waiter.

Modal (future time)*	Meaning(s)
will be able to/won't be able to; will be unable to	(1) ability; (2) possibility or potential
can/can't	no separate future form, but shows future ability when used with words like *next, tomorrow,* etc.—see *will be able to*
could/couldn't	(1), (2), and (4), use *will be able to* for future; (3) no change when asking permission or making requests for future situations with words like *next, tomorrow,* etc.; (5) no change to use with future possibility in certain situations (used with *if* or *unless*)

had better/had better not	no change, but is also used for future situations with words like *next, tomorrow,* etc.
have got to/haven't got to	no change, but is also used for future situations with words like *next, tomorrow,* etc.; usually replaced by will *have to*
will have to/won't have to	necessity (replaces *have got to* and *must* in future situations)
like to/like to	enjoyment—special form for future
may/may not	(1) possible future situation; (2) asking or giving permission for future actions; (3) discuss possible explanations for future behavior or situations
might/might not	(1) not used for future; (2) doubtful future situation; (3) asking permission (very polite) for future action—negative not used
must/don't (doesn't) have to/don't (doesn't) need to	(1) and (2) no separate future form—see *will have to*
will need to/won't need to	requirement (usually personal)
ought to/ought not	(1) advice; (2) hinted responsibility or duty; no change, but is also used for future situations with words like *next, tomorrow,* etc.
should/shouldn't	(1), (2), and (3) no change, but is also used for some future situations with words like *next, tomorrow,* etc.
will want to/won't want to	wishing; talking about preferences; limited use in future situations
will/won't	(1) definite future intent; (2) prediction about future; (3) and (4) no separate future form—use *would* negative form rarely used for (3) and (4)
would/wouldn't	(1) not used; (2) discussion of doubtful future event; (3) polite requests; (4) offering or inviting**

THE DETAILS

Will you *be able to <u>carry</u>* those packages?

Tony *could <u>earn</u>* $100,000 a year if he gets his graduate degree.

I*'ll have to <u>leave</u>* the party early this Saturday—I*'ve got to <u>be</u>* on the golf course at 8:00 on Sunday.

I *may <u>fly</u>* to Brussels next week if necessary.

Would Bobby *like to <u>come</u>* with us next Saturday?

John *should <u>return</u>* from Iowa on the 28th of next month.

Will David still *want to <u>become</u>* an actor after going to some auditions?

Note: *We usually use *will* with modals for future situations, but in most cases *be going to* can also be used.

Note: **When we are making an offer or inviting someone for a future event, we usually use *Would you* (*he, she,* etc.) *like to* . . . ? or *I would* (*'d*) *like it if you* (*he, she,* etc.). . . .

You*'ll like <u>being</u>* in England for Christmas.

Tom *won't like <u>working</u>* with his new boss.

Comparing Things

a. Comparing nouns

Comparing things is an important part of every language. When we compare nouns in English, there can be either exactly (or almost exactly) equal quantities of each or there will be less of one and more of the other. When we compare quantities of nouns that we think will be more or less equal, we use *as much . . . as/as many . . . as* (or *as little . . . as/as few . . . as* if we consider the quantities to be small). We use *as much . . . as/as little . . . as* for noncountable nouns, and *as many . . . as/as few . . . as* for countable nouns. This is called an *equal* comparison.

Mary has $50. **Angela also has $50.**	→→→	**Mary has *as much* money *as* Angela.**
Mary drinks wine only once a year. Angela also drinks wine only once a year.	→→→	**Mary drinks *as little* wine *as* Angela.**
Anthony has 10 neckties. **Paul also has 10 neckties.**	→→→	**Anthony has *as many* neckties *as* Paul.**
Anthony has only two belts. **Paul also has only two belts.**	→→→	**Anthony has *as few* belts *as* Paul.**

If the amounts are exactly the same (not just *almost* exactly), we can reverse equal comparisons.

Paul has *as many* neckties *as* Anthony. BUT		
Anthony has 11 neckties. **Paul has 10 neckties.**	→→→	**Paul *doesn't* have *quite as many* neckties *as* Anthony.**

THE DETAILS

If the exact amount isn't really important, only the fact that the amounts are very close, we can say *about* as *much/many* (we don't use *about* with *little/few*).

Dan has _about_ as much work as (he had) last year at this time.
Both my kids have _about_ as many colds as the average.

Comparing nouns is one of the areas in English conversation where we need an accurate understanding of the difference between noncountable nouns and countable nouns. If you want to review them, see Chapter 6, sections a and b.

Henry drinks *as much* coffee *as* Ed (does).

Janet eats *as many* cookies *as* Rhonda (does), but she doesn't eat *as much* ice cream *as* Rhonda (does).

Edmund doesn't like *as much* ice in his drinks *as* Jackie (does).

There is *as much* snow in January *as* (there is) in February.

There aren't *as many* farms around here *as* there were in my childhood.

The newspaper claims that they have *as much* oil in Alaska *as* in the North Sea. (claims = says)

The newspaper forgot to add that they don't have *as many* oil wells in Alaska *as* (they do) in the North Sea.

For asking questions with equal comparisons, we usually use a yes/no format.

Was Andrew married *as many* years *as* Sarah (was)?
Does Uncle Harold eat *as much as* Grandpa did?*   (= as much food)

Note: *When the two things we are comparing have different time frames, we usually include at least the second helping verb, or even the actual second verb.

Ted plays as much basketball now as he _did_ in high school. (= now vs. "then")

Ted plays as much basketball as Bill (_does_). (= both halves are "now")

It is possible, however, to ask open-ended questions by using *How much/many . . . compared to . . . ?* when you have no idea about the answer.

How much rice do the Japanese eat *compared to* the Chinese?

How many taxis are there in New York *compared to* Paris?

To compare quantities of nouns that we think will probably *not* be equal, we use *more . . . than . . . /less . . . than . . .* for non-countable nouns (or *more . . . than . . . /fewer . . . than . . .* for countable nouns). This is an *unequal* comparison.

In our family, we eat *more* fish *than* (we eat) red meat.

There's always *less* water pressure in the evening *than* in the morning.

Donny's father has *more* hair *than* my father (has).

Anne complains about her sisters *more than* her brothers.

There are *fewer* weeds in Burt's garden *than* in ours.

Sandy has *more* CDs *than* I (do), but *fewer* cassettes.*

There are *more* subway seats available on the weekends *than* (there are) during the week.

Note: *You may hear some native speakers say "more than *me* (*him/us/them*)," but this is still nonstandard in most situations. The accepted form is still *more than I* (*he/we/they*).

THE DETAILS

b. Comparing adjectives and adverbs

When we compare nouns, we are comparing the quantity of the nouns. When we compare adjectives, we are comparing the "quantity" of the characteristic the adjective is describing. In the case of adverbs, we are comparing the way that the subject does something. For equal comparisons, we again use the *as . . . as* structure, but instead of *much/many; little/few*, we use *as . . . (big/pretty/hot/expensive/quickly/hard/delicious) as*.

Henry drinks as much coffee as Ed, but he doesn't make it *as strong as* Ed does. (= as Ed makes coffee)

I think this TV show is almost *as boring as* my high school algebra class.

In another few years, Eva will be almost *as pretty as* her mother.

Those parrots are *as noisy as* my brothers.

Larry has to work *as hard* now *as* he did 15 years ago.

It's going to be *as hot* next week *as* it has been this week.

There are three forms that adjectives and adverbs take in unequal comparisons.

- Most one-syllable adjectives and many two-syllable adjectives add *-er*.

- All the one-syllable adverbs (usually the ones that are spelled and pronounced the same way as certain adjectives: *early, late, fast, straight, hard,* * *high, low, free, long,* etc.) also add *-er*, but *-ly* adverbs use the *more . . . than/less . . . than* structure (*fewer . . . than* is used only for comparisons of nouns, not adjectives or adverbs).

- Many two- and three-syllable adjectives also use *more . . . than/less . . . than* for unequal comparisons (a few can use either form). Finally, a few adjectives and adverbs are irregular in comparisons.

Note: *The word *hard* can be either an adjective or an adverb when it means "difficult" or "with endurance" (This test isn't easy, it's *hard;* My father works *hard*). When we use *hard* as the opposite of *soft* (This mattress is *hard*), it can only be an adjective.

Adjective/Adverb	Comparative: *-er*
angry	angr**ier***
big	big**ger***
cheap	cheap**er**
few	few**er**
fat	fat**ter***
happy	happ**ier***
hard	hard**er**
healthy	health**ier***
long	long**er**
loud	loud**er**
new	new**er**
old	old**er**
poor	poor**er**
sad	sad**der***
short	short**er**
slow	slow**er**
small	small**er**
strong	strong**er**
thick	thick**er**
thin	thin**ner***
tough	tough**er**
wide	wid**er**

Note: *There are certain English spelling changes (final *-y* →→→ *-i*, for example) that affect these adjectives and adverbs (see Chapter 1, section c, *Nouns—one or more*, for details).

David's *thinner than* (he was) the last time we met—is he all right?

This steak seems *tougher than* stew meat, but maybe my teeth are weaker *than* they used to be.**

THE DETAILS

My parents were *angrier than* I've ever seen them before.
Show me a slightly *smaller* size *than* this, would you?
This is *harder than* I thought (it would be).
A cat's fur is *softer than* a dog's, but its tongue is *rougher*.
It's been *cloudier* this month *than* I've ever seen it before.

Note: **If we compare a person's habit, mood, or situation "now" with his or her past, we often use the phrase (*than*) . . . *used to* (*be/do/have*, etc.). In most such cases, we usually can't leave the verb out the way we can with helping verbs—especially if we give the reason for the change.

Adjective/Adverb	Comparative: *more/less*
afraid	**more** afraid
beautiful/ beautifully	**more** beautiful/ beautifully
careful/carefully	**more** careful/carefully
complicated	**more** complicated
delicious	**more** delicious
difficult	**more** difficult
enjoyable	**more** enjoyable
exciting	**more** exciting
expensive	**more** expensive
important	**more** important
handsome	**more** handsome*
intelligent	**more** intelligent
painful	**more** painful
quiet	**more** quiet*
unhappy	**more** unhappy*/**
stupid	**more** stupid
slowly	**more** slowly
thoroughly	**more** thoroughly

Note: *These can be either *-er* or the *more . . . than/less . . . than* form. Other such adjectives and adverbs include *gentle, narrow, polite,* and *simple*.

Note: **Very often, an adjective or adverb and its opposite will follow different forms in comparisons: happy →→→ happ*ier*; unhappy →→→ *more* unhappy. Although we can also say *unhappier,* we can't say *more happy*.

The soloist sang even *more beautifully than* last time.

Darren seems to be *less intelligent than* his brother.

Ellen works *harder,* but *less effectively than* she used to (work).

Personally, I think the ballet is *more entertaining than* opera.

On the other hand, opera is *more enjoyable* on TV *than* ballet (is).

We're *less worried* about money now *than* we were before.

Since his retirement, Carl's moods change *more frequently,* and he's been *more difficult than* ever.

Adjective/Adverb	Irregular Comparative
bad/badly	worse
good/well	better
far	farther/further***
little	less
much/many	more

Note: ***Farther* means "a greater distance," but *further* means "continued" or "additional."

Steve has to travel 30 minutes *farther* to his new office than he did to his old one. (more distance)

The professor will have to do *further* research before he can publish his findings. (additional studies)

Andrew is a very good skier, but Ted really is *better* (*than* Andrew is).

THE DETAILS

Ted skis far *better than* any of the others in his group.

I feel *worse* today *than* yesterday, and my fever is *higher,* too.

We use certain words, called intensifiers, to emphasize the degree of sameness or difference in comparisons. These intensifiers help the listener understand how close or unequal the quantities or qualities in the comparison are.

For equal comparisons (*as . . . as*), we use the intensifiers *exactly, quite,* and *just* to show that there is no (or almost no) difference between the two parts of the comparison, or *almost, not quite, not nearly,* or *hardly** to show a greater degree of difference. A special case is the intensifier *at least,** which makes the listener think that there is a greater positive, not negative or neutral, difference—in the speaker's opinion, of course.

For unequal comparisons (*more . . . than, less . . . than*), we use these intensifiers: *a bit, somewhat, considerably, much/a lot/far* (*more . . . /less . . . than*), or (*more/less . . . than*) *ever.* With superlatives (see section c), we often use (*the . . . -est*) *by far, of all,* or *ever,* to show how far above (or below) the others in the comparison the subject is.

Note: *These intensifiers are all given in order from the smallest to the greatest degree of difference.

Linda is <u>at least</u> *as beautiful as* Jeanne. (more beautiful than Jeanne—big *positive* difference)

The weather <u>isn't nearly</u> *as bad* here *as* (it is) in the northern part of the state. (big *negative* difference)

This hotel is <u>far</u> *nicer than* the one we stayed in last year.

Mark looks <u>considerably</u> *older than* the last time we met.

John is <u>somewhat</u> *better off than* before his stocks increased in value. (well off = financially prosperous)

The new medicine was a mistake—I feel *worse than* <u>ever</u>.

c. Superlatives—the best, the most, etc.

Equal and unequal comparisons compare one thing (or group of things) to another specific thing. We can also compare one thing (or group of things) to everything else in the same category. This is called a *superlative*. When we say an actor is *the best,* or a restaurant is *the worst,* we are using a superlative to place the actor higher than all other actors, or to place a particular restaurant below all other restaurants.

For superlatives of adjectives or adverbs, we use either *the . . . -est,* or *the most/least . . . .* The rules follow those explained for comparisons of adjectives and adverbs. If the adjective or adverb forms the comparison with *-er,* then the superlative will follow the same pattern. With superlatives (formed with *-est*), we always use *the* as part of the structure.

Superlatives: -est form

the angri**est**

the big**gest**

the cheap**est**

the few**est**

the fat**test**

the happi**est**

the healthi**est**

the hard**est**

the long**est**

the loud**est**

the new**est**

the old**est**

the sad**dest**

the short**est**

the small**est**

the strong**est**

the thick**est**

the thin**nest**

the tough**est**

the wid**est**

THE DETAILS

My great-grandmother is *the oldest* woman in this town.

That was *the loudest* rock concert I ever went to.

I'm going to make Larry *the thickest, juiciest* steak I can find on his birthday.*

Tell me what dish on the menu has *the fewest* calories—I'm dieting.

Charley has *the greenest* lawn—how does he do it? (the deepest/brightest green color)

Susan has *the nicest* eyes and *the prettiest* smile of any girl I know.

Is this *the cheapest* place you could find?

I wore my *newest* outfit to the party.**

Note: *If we use two superlatives together, we can leave out the second *the*—although we can use it if we prefer.

Note: **If we use a possessive (see Chapter 1, section d, *Noun substitutes—possessives and pronouns*), we don't use *the* with the superlative.

Superlatives: *the most/least*
the most afraid
the most angry
the most beautiful/beautifully
the most careful/carefully
the most common*
the most complicated
the most delicious
the most difficult
the most enjoyable
the most exciting
the most expensive
the most handsome*
the most important
the most intelligent

the most painful
the most poorly
the most quiet*
the most slowly
the most stupid
the most thoroughly
the most unhappy*

Note: *The same adjectives and adverbs that can be formed with both *-er* and *more/less* (see section b), have superlative forms that can be used with either *-est* or *the most/least.*

That was *the most delicious* roast duck—even *more delicious than* my mother's.
I hate this author's mysteries—they have *the most complicated, least interesting* storylines.
Dad's arthritis is *the most painful* in damp weather.
That's *the saddest, most horrible* story I've ever heard.
We're going to Mallorca at *the sunniest* time of year.

Adjective/Adverb	Comparative	Superlative
bad/badly	worse	the worst
good/well	better	the best
far	farther/further	the farthest/furthest
little	less	the least
much/many	more	the most

Paul is *the worst* golfer I know.
Why did you choose *the most* expensive hotel?
Tony told me that this is *the best* fish restaurant in the city, but these clams are *the worst* I've ever had.

Too/Enough

a. Enough/not enough *with nouns*

The word *enough* is used to show that something exists in an adequate amount, or that an action has been done adequately. If the speaker thinks that the amount or degree of something is less than adequate, he or she will use <u>not</u> enough.

There's *enough wood* on the fire—don't add any more.

I think Sally put *enough salt* in the soup.

That movie does*n't* have *enough suspense*.

I did*n't* bring *enough cash* with me—do you have *enough* to lend me $20?

The coach at the high school said Ted had *enough speed and agility* to win the marathon.

The noun always follows *enough,* even in questions.

b. Enough *with adjectives and adverbs*

In the previous examples, *enough* was used with nouns, but it can also be used with adjectives and adverbs.

This room is *good enough.*

Is it *warm enough* for you?

The green armchair is pretty, but it's *not comfortable enough.*

We didn't get here *early enough*—all the good seats are gone.

The wine isn't *cold enough.*

As you can see in the examples, *enough* comes before nouns, but after adjectives or adverbs.

c. Too much/too many *with nouns*

If we want to show that we think the amount or degree of something *exceeds* the perfect level instead of falling below it, we use *too much* with noncountable nouns, and *too many* with countable nouns.

There's *too much noise* in this room.

There are *too many people* in this restaurant.

Carl spends *too much time* with his dogs.

I know I have *too many suits,* but I need them for work.

Too/enough always shows the speaker's *opinion* (or the speaker talking about another person's opinion), very rarely a "universal" standard—even when the majority agree with that opinion. *Too much/many . . .* and *not enough . . .* are really very close in meaning, but one emphasizes the excess of negative, the other emphasizes the lack of positive. The same is true of saying that there *is too little/are too few* of something; it's the same as saying that there *isn't enough* of something. If we say that there is *more than enough* of something we usually mean that the amount of something is excessive, even if the basic situation isn't bad in itself.

(less than "perfect")	("perfect")	(more than "perfect")
↓	↓	↓
(not enough . . .)	(enough . . .)	(more than enough)
(too little/few . . .)	(<u>not</u> too much/ too little/few)	(too much/many . . .)

Jackie has *more than enough* clothes.

Jackie doesn*'t* have *enough* shoes.

Jackie has *too few* shoes.

Tom has *more than enough* work.

Tom *never* has *enough* time.*

Tom has *too little* time.

THE DETAILS

We've had *more than enough* sun this year.
We haven*'t* had *enough rain* this year.
We've had *too little rain* this year.

Larry is spending *more than enough* time with Vivien.
Larry is*n't* spending *enough* time with Jill.
Larry is spending *too much time* with Vivien.

Note: *Never* can substitute for *not* if a situation is constant, daily, or habitual.

d. Too *with adverbs and adjectives*

Most often, in addition to being used with nouns, *too* is used in sentences with adjectives or adverbs. Although adverbs and adjectives always come before *enough*, they always follow *too*—even in questions. This is the typical word order:

- Affirmative sentences: **too <u>hot</u>, too <u>slowly</u>, <u>hot</u> enough, <u>fast</u> enough**

- Negative sentences: **<u>not</u> too hot, <u>not</u> too slowly, <u>not</u> hot enough, <u>not</u> fast enough**

- Questions: **<u>is</u> . . . too hot? <u>is</u> . . . too slowly? <u>is</u> . . . hot enough? <u>is</u> . . . fast enough?**

Is the coffee *sweet enough* for Linda?

Barbara changes her mind *too often.*

Mary's Italian was*n't* *fluent enough* to be helpful on our trip to Florence.

It's *too cold* to go swimming.

The architect did*n't* draw the plans *accurately enough.*

Is it *too late* in the season for skiing?

Tina did*n't* vacuum the living room *thoroughly enough.*

Sean, the stereo is *too loud.*

e. Too/enough *with infinitive verbs and phrases*

Too/enough can often be followed by a verb or phrase that gives the reason the speaker feels there is *too much* or *not enough* of something. The verbs and verb phrases in the following examples are underlined:

Carl does*n't* spend *enough time* with the children <u>to understand them</u>.

The car has *enough gas* <u>to get to the office and back</u>.

Do Bill and Tammy have *enough money* <u>to last until pay day</u>?

The board feels Dr. Maitland does*n't* have *enough experience* <u>to run the department</u>.

Harry talks *too much* <u>to be a good dinner companion</u>.

There's *too much food* here <u>to eat at one meal</u>.

This soup has *too many calories* <u>to be good for dieters</u>.

Tony Clark has *too many enemies* <u>to become the firm's president</u>.

If the speaker wants to emphasize that something is exactly enough, the word *just* is used before *enough. Just* should only occasionally be used in sentences with *too* because it sounds critical, impatient, or forceful. *Just* is seldom used together with *not* in *too/enough* sentences, but there are a few exceptions.

Ed's "best" is *just not enough* for this assignment.   ("best" = best efforts; just not enough = just not good enough/ not sufficient)

You have *just enough time* to get to work (if you leave now).

There's *just enough milk* left for breakfast tomorrow.

Bob has *just enough skill* to do his job well.

There are *just too many people* here—I'm leaving!

There *just* are*n't enough hours* in the day for all this work!

If the speaker wants to show that a statement is not an absolute, but is his or her personal judgment (or the subjective opinion of another person), *for* is used along with either a proper name or

141

THE DETAILS

an object pronoun (*me/him/her/us,* etc.—see Chapter 1, section d, *Noun substitutes—possessives and pronouns*).

This is *too much homework for Bobby* to do in one night.	(= but not for his brother)
There isn't *enough time <u>for me</u>* to read the paper in the mornings.	(= but my wife can read it in 15 minutes)
That house costs too much <u>for us</u> to afford right now.	(= but my supervisor can afford it)
It's not warm enough <u>for Grandpa</u> to sit outside today.	(= but the rest of the family thinks it's perfect)
Is Helen athletic enough <u>for George</u>?	(= but maybe George doesn't care)
This coffee is too hot <u>for me</u> to drink.	(= but my father likes his coffee boiling hot)
The suitcases are too heavy <u>for Sue</u> to lift by herself.	(= but her brother can lift them with one hand)

Some final points to remember:

- Since the speaker always uses *enough* in a (relatively or absolutely) positive sense, it should be used only with adjectives and adverbs that represent positive characteristics or behavior; for something actually or potentially negative, use *not . . . enough* (with a positive adjective or adverb) or *too* (with a negative adjective or adverb).

Terry is a <u>careful</u> driver.	(= good behavior)
Terry always drives carefully.	
Paul is a *careful enough* driver in city traffic, but he is*n't* really *careful enough* on the highways.	
Paul drives *carefully enough* to avoid accidents.	
Dan is a <u>fast</u> and <u>reckless</u> driver.	(= bad behavior)
Dan drives *too fast* and *recklessly* for me to ride with him.	

- Don't confuse the use of *very* with *too*. *Very* just means "a lot", *too* means "more than is good/suitable/acceptable/wise, etc."

Eve is *very* clever.	(= high degree of cleverness)
Eve is *too* clever.	(= her cleverness will cause problems)
It's *very* breezy today.	(= the breeze is strong)
It's *too* breezy today—some of my flowers have broken off.	(= the breeze is so strong it's damaging)

143

10 Building Sentences

a. Making verbs and nouns agree

English, like most Western languages, has both singular and plural forms for nouns (*book/book<u>s</u>; child/child<u>ren</u>*) and pronouns (*I/ <u>we</u>; he, she, it/<u>they</u>;* etc.). It also has some changes in verbs (in only certain tenses) that show whether a subject is singular or plural. For helping verbs, the present and past tenses are *I <u>am</u> reading/they <u>are</u> reading; you <u>have</u> seen/he <u>has</u> seen,* etc. For full verbs, the present tenses are *he go<u>es</u>/they go; she say<u>s</u>/I say; he catch<u>es</u>/we catch,* etc., all depending on whether the subject is singular or plural.

One of the strictest rules in English is that a singular subject must have a singular verb, and a plural subject must have a plural verb (this is called *subject/verb agreement*). When we make simple sentences, the choices are quite easy: *Mickey <u>has</u> a family,* not *Mickey <u>have</u> a family.* When we build slightly more complex sentences, however, the choices also become more complex: Is it *The family <u>go</u> to the beach,* or *the family <u>goes</u>* . . . ? Do we say *Politics <u>is</u> complex,* or *Politics <u>are</u>* . . . ? Which do we choose: *Either Bill or his brothers <u>is</u> going to play tennis,* or *Either Bill or his brothers <u>are</u> going to play* . . . ?

Many of these choices are easy after you know the "rules," but some are harder. This is because some subjects that seem singular (no final -s or other typical plural form) are considered plural, and *so must take a plural verb,* whereas other subjects that our logic tells us "should" be plural are treated as singular and take singular verbs. Still others take either a singular or plural verb, depending on how we use the word. There are very few real rules, but here are some general guidelines. Remember that the only *real* rule is that if a subject (usually, but not always, a noun) has both singular and plural forms, the verb *must* agree with the form that is used in the sentence. When other words or structures make the sentence more complex, or make the verb's subject harder to identify, this isn't always as easy as it seems.

The house**s** on this street **_are_** **all** painted gray.
One **of** the houses on this street **_is_** painted gray.

Those boy**s** over there **_are_** Finnish.
That boy over there **_is_** Finnish.

Who **_is_** there?*
Do you know who **those** girl**s** standing over there **_are_**?

Note: *This is used when you ask the identity of a person (or maybe *several people*) you can't see—when your doorbell or intercom rings but you can't see outside, for example.

These subjects take singular verbs:

- Proper nouns for corporations and for religious, military, government, or other official institutions

The Navy accept**s** people 18 years or older.
Congress expect**s** to pass the new law by March 1st.
Is General Motors recalling one of **_its_** models?*
Buddhism **_has_** always discouraged materialism.

Note: *This is true only for American English. Speakers of British English usually use a *plural* verb for businesses or other official groups, or for sports teams (*Sotheby's* *have* *announced . . . ; The Tory Party* *are* *intending to . . . ; Middlesex* *win* *by . . . ,* etc.).

- Most nouns that represent a group of people or animals (only when they are acting as a group, not individually)

The herd of cattle **_is_** being driven across the plains.	(BUT *The cattle* *are . . .*)
The swarm of killer bees **_attacks_** when **_it_** **_is_** disturbed by loud sounds.	(BUT *The bees* *attack . . .* *they . . .* *are . . .*)

145

THE DETAILS

The public *is* eager for news of the reforms.	(BUT *Members of the public are* . . .)
The orchestra *begins* by tuning *its* instruments.	(BUT *The orchestra members/ musicians begin* . . .)
The class *has* decided to participate in the event.	(BUT *The students have* . . .)
My family *likes* to eat dinner early.	(BUT *My wife and children like* . . .)
The board of directors *is* going to announce plans for restructuring.	(BUT *The members of the board are going to* . . .)

Other such subjects include the audience, the committee, the company, the couple (the couple = two people living together; *The couple that lives next door* . . . , etc.), the government, the group, the jury, the majority, the management, the population, the team.

Be careful: Any phrase with the subject *a couple of -s* takes a plural, not a singular, verb (*A couple of bottles of beer are broken,* etc.).

- most nouns that represent a concept, principle, moral belief, or emotion

Anger *is* a destructive emotion.	
Freedom *has* many meanings.	
Truth *exists* separately from justice.	
Trouble *comes* in many forms.	(trouble = a difficult situation; troubles = various problems)
My experience with the police *is* limited.	(experience = personal knowledge; experiences = events that have happened to someone)

BUILDING SENTENCES

- noncountable nouns

Money *is* less important than friendship.
The fog *has* begun to move in.
The cold *penetrates* into all my bones.   (= cold weather)
High humidity *makes* people tired.   (= humid weather)
Janet's jewelry *has* been stolen.
Success *isn't* always easy to measure.
Car insurance *is* getting very expensive nowadays.

- most serious diseases (not minor problems like colds, headaches, etc.)

Cancer *is* still the main risk for smokers, but heart disease *ranks* as number two.
Tuberculosis *has* started to increase again.
AIDS *costs* government and insurance companies billions of dollars a year.
Depression *is* now treatable with medication.

- academic subjects or words that end in *-ics*

Logic *is* one of the subjects the ancient Greeks studied.
Jim says, mathematics *is* interesting, but arithmetic *is* dull.
Does anybody understand what "ethics" *means*?
Athletics often *provides* many students with scholarships.
Economics *has* always been a compulsory subject for all students of business.

THE DETAILS

Some people think statistics _is_ boring.

(= a boring subject to study; BUT _These_ statistics _are_ alarming, etc.)

Words that end in -ics can also be used with plural verbs if we are talking about a <u>specific</u> case: _his politics <u>are</u>_ . . . = his political ideas; _their ethics <u>are</u>_ . . . = their ethical standards, etc.

When we say "the Olympics," we really mean _the Olympic Games,_ so it always takes a plural, not singular verb.

Politics <u>has</u> a bad reputation.

- measurements, amounts of money, amounts of numerical units, formulas in arithmetic, or lengths of time as units

As I recall, 2.4 inches _<u>is</u>_ 5 centimeters.

(BUT _There <u>are</u> 2.4 inches in 5 centimeters._)

Five hundred dollars _<u>buys</u>_ a lot less than it used to.

A hundred and twenty dollars _<u>was</u>_ missing from my account last month.

Two boxes of shirts plus three boxes of dresses _makes_ five boxes of clothes.

I think eighteen hours _<u>is</u>_ a long time to be sitting on a plane.

(BUT _There <u>are</u> 24 hours in a day)_

Two dozen _<u>is</u>_ all we need.

(BUT _A dozen eggs <u>are</u> broken)_

A few minutes _<u>is</u>_ enough time to say what I want to (say).

Ten minutes _<u>is</u>_ all I've waited.

(= I've only waited 10 minutes)

- individual sports and games

Chess *demands* concentration.
Tennis always *attracts* big crowds.
Dominoes *is* a lot of fun.
Darts *is* taken very seriously in Britain.
Checkers *has* lost a lot of *its* popularity.

- sports teams that we identify by their home city or with a team name that doesn't end in -*s*. (See below for treatment of team names that do end in -*s*.)

Next week New York *plays* Miami in the finals.
Fans cheer as Hamburg *scores* a big win!

Other subjects that always take a singular verb include: a collection (of) -*s* (a collection of doll*s*, a collection of dish*es*, etc.); a pair (of) -*s* (a pair of shoe*s*, a pair of pistol*s*); a set (of) -*s* (a set of kni*ves*, a set of old coin*s*).

These subjects take plural verbs:

- Nouns that have no real singular form (see Chapter 3, section g, *There is/there are,* for more about this type of noun)

I think your glasses *are* in the car.
We can't tell you the contents of the will—*they're* secret.
***Those* pants *are* too long—have your tailor fix *them*.**
***These* scissors *are* dull.**
My old clothes *are* going to go to charity.
Bob's savings *have* been used up, and his other assets *are* only his car and stereo.
Your thanks *are* all the "payment" I need.

THE DETAILS

- All sports teams and musical groups with names that end in -s

The New York Yankees *are* playing well tonight.
Fans are disappointed that the Padres *have* lost so many games.
The Beatles *are* still popular.
The Rolling Stones *are* touring again this summer.

These subjects may take either singular or plural verbs, depending on what the speaker means:

the police = policemen/police officers—plural
the police = the police force—singular

sports = the category of sports; athletics—singular
sports = different sports—plural

Fractions can take either singular or plural verbs, depending on whether the subject is a noncountable or countable noun.

A half a crate of pears *is* too much fruit. (½)
One-half of the pears *are* ripe. (½)
I think one-fourth of the wine *is* enough for the stew. (¼)
A quarter of the students *have* joined the club. (¼)
One-third of the flour *is* for another purpose. (⅓)
Only two-fifths of the land *is* suitable for food crops. (⅖)
Four-fifths of the employees *are* part-time workers. (⅘)

These words are usually used with singular subjects or verbs:

- someone, something, somewhere, anyone, anything, anywhere, everyone, everything, everywhere, no one, nothing, nowhere*

There _is_ something I want to discuss with you.   (BUT _There are some things_ . . .)

I shouldn't park here, but everyone _does_ it.

_Is_ there anywhere else we can sit?

Nothing get_s_ done around here!   (gets done = is completed)

Note: *If we use the words _some_ and _any_ alone, they almost always go with a plural subject and verb.

- either/neither

Neither of them _is_ a good driver.

Either of the computers _works_ well.

- each/every

Every child _has_ to take this placement test.

Each of Mark's shirts _hangs_ on _its_ own hanger.

- the majority

In a democracy, the majority _rules_.

The majority _has_ made _its_ wishes clear.

THE DETAILS

Majority takes a singular verb only if it represents a group; but if sentences use *a* instead of *the,* and if they have *of* followed by a noun or pronoun, we can usually expect them to take a plural verb (a̱ majority o̱f the employee̱s *are* against it; a̱ majority o̱f u̱s *think* that . . . , etc.). This rule also applies to *the/a couple, the/a number,* and *the/a total.* With *the/a number* and *the/a total,* however, using *of* doesn't change the need for a singular verb. Only the article *a* together with *of -s̱* needs a plural verb.

- the couple (people only; animals and things use *a couple of -s* + plural verb)

The couple in the apartment above mine i̱s always fighting.
(BUT *A couple of dogs a̱re on the lawn;* the̱ couple = romantically connected people; a̱ couple = two -s̱)

- the total

The total for your purchases *come̱s* to $29.45.
The total of the CEO's salary for five years *equaḻs* one-third of our net profits. (BUT *A total o̱f 17 people we̱re killed in the accident*)

- the number

The number of crimes in this neighborhood i̱s declining.
(declining = going down)
The number of high school students who leave school before graduation *amaze̱s* me. (amazes = surprises very much; BUT *A number of them do̱n't find jobs easily*)

- from/to

From two to three years *ha̱s* been the average time to complete this study program.
The doctor said that from ten days to two weeks i̱s going to be needed for Pam's recovery from the operation.

- this/that kind (sort, type) of

This kind of sky always *means* rain.
That sort of car *has* always appealed to me. (appealed to = interested; tempted)
This type of problem *is* exactly what we hoped to avoid.
That kind of energetic person always *makes* me tired.

- part of

Part of his stock *has* to go to the government for taxes.
Part of the money *is* already in the bank.

These words are usually used with plural subjects or verbs:

- both

Both of these books *are* popular.
Both children *have* nightmares.
I like David and Elizabeth, but both of them *talk* too much.
Both coffee and tea *give* me a headache.

- between (always followed by a plural subject)

Charles will be away between the first and the third weeks in March. (BUT *Charles will be away from the first to third week in March*)
Just between *us*, I hate spicy food.
It takes between 30 and 45 minutes to make this cake.

THE DETAILS

These words can be used with either singular or plural subjects and verbs. If the subject is a noncountable noun, it takes a singular verb; if it's a countable noun, it takes a plural verb. This "rule" is followed before any other.

- these/those kind<u>s</u>, (sort<u>s</u>, type<u>s</u>) of -s

---

These kind<u>s</u> of <u>people</u> _are_ often unstable. (BUT *This kind of person _is_ often unstable*)
Those sort<u>s</u> of movie<u>s</u> _make_ the children overexcited. (This sort . . . *makes* . . .)
Those type<u>s</u> of desserts _aren't_ my favorites. (This type . . . *is* . . .)

- all

All of the wine _is_ warm.
All of these book<u>s</u> _are_ mine.
All the children _have gone_ home.

- some, any, no, none

Some people _are_ very kind.
Any house _is_ going to need repairs.
Are any of the report<u>s</u> for March available?
I think there _is_ some soup on the stove, but there _are_ no potatoe<u>s</u>.
None of the fruit _is_ fresh.

- half of

Half of the fraternity _is_ at the football game now.
Half of the members _are_ in a meeting.

- a/the percentage of

The percentage of silk _is_ very small in this fabric.
A percentage of the profits _go_ to charity.

- along with

The boys, along with their sister, _were_ hurt in the accident.
The snow, along with the icy winds, _has_ finally stopped.

- as well as

The soldiers, as well as their general, _have_ returned from the front.
The ocean, as well as the clouds, _was_ promising a bad storm.

- together with

Ted's driver's license, together with his keys, his money, and all his credit cards, _was_ stolen.
The vice-president of sales and the head accountant, together with the entire company, _were_ surprised by the news.

Note: *The subject always comes first with all three of these patterns, and the verb agrees with it, even if several other nouns come between the subject and the verb.

- either . . . or . . . /neither . . . nor . . . *

Neither his mother nor his two aunts _are_ at home now. (BUT _Joe is neither clever nor charming_)
Either eggs or cereal sounds good to me. (cereal _is_ . . . ; BUT _Either cereal or eggs sound_ . . .)

THE DETAILS

Note: ** Either . . . or . . . /neither . . . nor . . .* always agrees with the subject closer to the verb. This is true even in questions.

b. Connecting things and thoughts—and, but, because, despite, etc.

At a certain point when we study a new language, we have to move away from the simple, one-concept sentences we have been using, and start to use grammar forms that will allow us to express our more complicated ideas. One of the first steps to making this happen is learning how to connect two (or more) separate but related ideas into one longer sentence. We often use a *connecting word* or words to do this.

There are several types of connecting words, divided into categories based on their specific purpose and on how they link ideas. Some connecting words tell the listener that the ideas are related in one of several different but still equal ways. Others are used when we want to show how one situation has affected the other, etc. In many cases, we link these concepts to explain or make clear our reason for doing something; in other cases, we explain the effect our actions have had, or will have, on another situation.

Each of these words is used in a slightly different way, both for their actual meaning and in the way we structure the sentence. To use many of them correctly, you need to understand the difference between a *clause* and a *phrase*. A clause (. . . *because <u>I wanted to go to the store</u>,* . . . ; . . . *as a result, <u>he has agreed to resign</u>*) is a group of words that can make sense alone—it has a subject and a verb. A phrase (*because of <u>the heavy rain</u>,* . . . ; *as a result of <u>his carelessness on the job</u>,* . . .) is just a group of words that "explain" a noun, verb, etc., but need the rest of the sentence to make sense. Some of these connecting words are used with certain clauses (there are many kinds of clauses), others are used with *noun phrases* (there are also several kinds of phrases), so it's useful to understand the difference between clauses and phrases. (Chapter 13 is all about clauses, so you will learn more about them later.)

Let's start with the simplest connecting words first. These words connect two or more equal ideas without showing any cause-and-effect relationship:

- and (shows a connection between things or ideas)

My dog is <u>brown</u> *and* <u>white</u>.
Tim has <u>a car</u>, <u>a motorcycle</u>, *and* <u>a bicycle</u>.*
These <u>hot days</u> *and* <u>cold nights</u> are bad for some plants.

Note: *When *and* connects three or more things, we separate the words with commas (,), putting *and* only before the last word in the series. We also do this with *but* and *or*.

- or (gives or shows a choice between two or more ideas)

Helen can be <u>as happy as a child</u> *or* <u>as sad as Hamlet</u>.
I can't decide whether <u>to take a vacation</u> *or* <u>buy new kitchen appliances</u>.

- but (introduces an idea that slightly disagrees with the word or words that come before it, so it is usually used with a negative)

They gave us <u>breakfast and lunch</u>, *but* they did<u>n't</u> give us <u>dinner</u>.**
The <u>rain stopped</u>, *but* <u>the sun didn't come out</u>.
Here's <u>Janet's phone number</u>, *but* <u>she's moving soon</u>.

Note: **Often, if the subject is the same, we just say *but not* . . . .

These words always connect two ideas basically in opposition to each other (notice the position of each of them in the examples):

- although/(even) though

Although he looks strong, his health isn't good.
Even though the Palmers live in a big house, they have no money in the bank.

THE DETAILS

- on the other hand/however***

Tom does have a lot of charm and good manners. *On the other hand,* his character isn't very good, and he has a terrible temper.

The marketing proposal sounds promising, and it may increase sales. *On the other hand,* it will cost a lot to put into operation.

Sarah usually cooks very well. *However,* she ruined last night's dinner.

Note: ***However* and *on the other hand* are completely interchangeable in meaning and sentence structure.

- while

While Tom has a lot of charm and good manners, his character isn't very good; and he has a terrible temper.

While the marketing proposal sounds promising, and may increase sales, it will cost a lot to put into operation.

These words show us that two people or things (1) share two characteristics, (2) share neither characteristic, or (3) share only one of two characteristics:

- too/so do (does)

Larry speaks French, and Danny does, *too.* (does = speaks French)

Larry speaks French, and *so does* Danny.

- neither (always used with a negative)

Paula does*n't* drive well, and *neither* does her husband.

- but not

Margaret is allergic to shellfish, *but not* (allergic) to fish.

These words show results or consequences:

- so

Mary wasn't home, *so* I left a note.
I forgot my umbrella, *so* I got wet.

- as a result (clause)/as a result *of* (noun/noun phrase)

The rain had turned to ice, and *as a result,* Betty lost control of the car.
Betty lost control of the car *as a result of* the icy road conditions.

- because (clause)/because of (noun/noun phrase)

***Because* John is so good-natured and handsome, he always has a lot of girlfriends.**
John always has a lot of girlfriends *because of* his good looks and his good-natured personality.

- due to the fact that (clause)/due to (noun/noun phrase)

***Due to the fact that* Deborah gives a good first impression, she gets a lot of job offers.**
Deborah gets a lot of job offers *due to* the good first impression she gives.

THE DETAILS

- since (can be used with either a clause or noun phrase)

Since you prefer meat, we're having steak for dinner.
Since it's your birthday, I baked a cake.

- in order to (verb phrase)

In order to be able to buy their house, Christina and Brad
borrowed money from his parents.

These words show overcoming obstacles or difficulties:

- despite/in spite of (noun phrase)

Despite his broken leg, David still attended the meeting.
In spite of his broken leg, David still attended the meeting.

- although/even though (clause)

Although he had a broken leg, David still attended the
meeting.
Even though he had a broken leg, David still attended the
meeting.

c. Cause and effect—simple sentences with *so* and *such*

We use the words *so* and *such* as an emphatic way to "under-
line" or strengthen our meaning. Although *such* is similar to
(but stronger than) *very*, *so* has to be followed by a result or
consequence. That is an important structural difference. Be
careful not to confuse this meaning of *so* with the connecting
word *so*, which means "*as a result of* . . . ."

Cats are *so beautiful,* but also *so unpredictable.*

Dan gets impatient with Billy *so often* because he (Billy) is *so terribly shy.*

Sandy spends *so much time* at the beauty parlor that she should be a professional model.

That is *such a nasty comment* to make about Sandy, and you've been friends for *such a long time.*

This is *such a lovely room*!

C
THE COMPLEX SENTENCE

11 When a Statement Is a Question

Most of the time, we use questions to get information. There are other types of "questions," however, that are really statements, even though we use them to subtly (1) find out how the listener feels about a subject—whether he or she agrees with us or not (these are called *tag questions*); (2) show surprise or mildly criticize the listener or another person (these are called *negative questions* because they always start with a negative); or (3) make a statement (*rhetorical questions*) without expecting an answer, or make an enthusiastic exclamation in question form (called *exclamation question*). Tag questions, the most common kind of "statement question," come in two types, positive and negative.

"normal" question:	***Do you* like steak?**
positive tag question:	**You *don't* like steak, *do you*?**
negative tag question:	**You *like* steak, *don't you*?**
negative question:	***Don't* you like steak?**
rhetorical question:	***Who doesn't* like steak?**
exclamation question:	***Don't* you like (*love*) steak!***

Note: *Although exclamation questions look like negative questions, there is quite a difference. See section c, *Rhetorical questions and exclamation questions.*

An important point to remember with these statement questions is that though most areas of English don't rely very heavily on tone of voice or intonation, all these questions—to varying degrees—need a particular intonation to match their structure.

We always use a *rising* intonation on the question tag when we want reassurance from the listener, or if we want the listener to deny or contradict some bad news.

WHEN A STATEMENT IS A QUESTION

[↗]

Blue Chip–stock prices didn't fall along with the others, *did*
***they*?**   [↗]

Harold's illness isn't really so serious, *is it*?

When we want *and expect* the listener to confirm information or facts, or to agree with an opinion or statement of ours, we use a *falling* intonation on the question tag.

[↘]

Carl's new wife seemed quite nice, didn't she?   [↘]

Tickets to Broadway shows are terribly expensive, aren't they?

There is another way to "ask" for the listener's agreement. In very informal English, when we want or expect the listener to agree with something, or to approve of a suggestion we are making *and that involves the listener*, we often add the words *right?* or *OK?* with a rising intonation to a statement or sometimes even to questions. We can use *right?* about factual information or about another person, but *OK?* is always about the listener's wishes, or the listener agreeing to the speaker's suggestion.

Roses like a sunny location, *right*? (= I'm sure you agree that this is true/that's correct information, isn't it?)

The movie is playing at the Cineplex, *right*? (= that is the correct theater, isn't it?)

Let's have dinner *after* the movie, OK? (= you don't mind if we eat after the movie rather than before, do you?)

How about going to that new Brazilian restaurant, *OK*? (= is that all right <u>with you</u>?)

a. Question tags

The way we form a tag question determines whether it is a positive or negative tag question. A tag question is a statement with the question part added separately at the end of the sentence. If the main verb of the sentence is an affirmative (*You* _live_ in New York . . .), the question tag must be negative (. . . _don't_ you?)—this is a _negative_ tag question. If the main verb of the sentence is a negative (_You don't live in New York . . ._), on the other hand, the question tag must be positive (. . . _do_ you?)—this is a _positive_ tag question. When we write a tag question, the question tag is always separated from the statement by a comma (,).

The first and most important thing to remember about tag questions is that whichever question tag you use, it _must be the opposite_ of, never the same as, the main verb of the sentence.

correct:	**You _live_ here, _don't_ you?**
correct:	**You _don't_ live here, _do_ you?**
incorrect:	**You _don't_ live here, _don't_ you?**

We can use any verb, modal, or helping verb—in all tenses—in tag questions.

It's hard to decide what to throw away, **isn't it?**

Sheila _teaches_ French, _doesn't she_?

Kevin _doesn't play_ golf very well, _does he_?

Corey and Meg _are studying_ medicine, _aren't they_?

Mark _was talking_ on the phone with his accountant, _wasn't he_?

You and Dan _will come_ to the party on Sunday, _won't you_?

The kids _aren't going to_ take the car tonight, _are they_?

Paul _hasn't received_ the birthday present I sent him yet, _has he_?

The paper _hadn't arrived_ by the time you left for the office yet, _had it_?

Modals are very frequently used in tag questions.

WHEN A STATEMENT IS A QUESTION

Grandma *wasn't able to* join the party, *was she*?

Jerry *can* speak French, *can't he*?

I suppose I *shouldn't park* here, *should I*?

Andrew *could* drive even as a teenager, *couldn't he*?

You really *want to go* to the baseball game, *don't you*?

It *would be* nice to have a vacation house, *wouldn't it*?

The subject (or pronoun) and verb in the statement, and the helping verb and pronoun in the question tag *must* agree in tense and number (see Chapter 10, section a, *Making verbs and nouns agree*).

correct:	*There* are two beds in the room, aren't *there*?
incorrect:	*There* are two beds in the room, aren't *they*?
correct:	*There are* two beds in the room, *aren't* there?
incorrect:	*There are* two beds in the room, *isn't* there?
correct:	Helen *has moved* to Chicago, *hasn't* she?
incorrect:	Helen *has moved* to Chicago, *didn't* she?

Tag questions have several different roles in English:

* to get some form of reassurance from the listener if we are unsure, or if we want another opinion—we especially use this when we want the listener to *deny* that some bad news is true (the first two examples)

Paula and John aren't really going to get a divorce, are they?	(= tell me that this isn't true)
Doctor, my mother will recover, won't she?	(= please tell me she won't die)

You (did) pay the bill before the 15th as I asked you to, didn't you? *

Granddad has been taking his medicine regularly, hasn't he?

- to "ask" the listener to confirm some information or fact that we already think is probably correct

---

The train leaves at 8:05, doesn't it?

You're an intern at the hospital, aren't you?

Roger's birthday is on the 15th, not the 14th, isn't it?

- to make sure the listener agrees with an opinion or evaluation we either have just given or are giving at that moment, or with a statement we either have just made or are making

---

That's right, isn't it?   (= what I just said was correct, wasn't it?)

Drivers who weave in and out of traffic like that are dangerous—aren't they?

Mike was awfully rude to that waiter just now, wasn't he?

I hate the combination of brown and yellow, don't you (hate it too)?**

Note: *The use of *did* in the statement part of this tag question is for emphasis. The speaker could simply have said *you paid . . . , didn't you*? instead.

Note: **This is one of the only times the question tag can have a different subject from the statement part of the tag question. It is very close to an exclamation question (see section c, *Rhetorical questions and exclamation questions*).

Our intonation is important here because we can use either a rising or a falling intonation on the question tag depending on our purpose.

b. Negative questions

This is another type of "question" that is really saying much more than it is asking. The question is always in the negative and always starts with the appropriate helping verb or modal.

We use negative questions for several things. The main purpose is to show that the speaker is surprised or even shocked

(*Weren't you supposed to get a promotion?* = *I'm surprised you didn't get a promotion*). Other uses of negative questions are

- to mildly, subtly, or strongly criticize
- to make a suggestion in an indirect way
- to remind the listener about doing something
- to show the speaker's impatience with a situation

Finally, there's a use that is *not* recommended: to subtly correct a mistake and to show off the speaker's knowledge (*Wasn't Zeus a Greek god rather than a Roman one?*).

Remember that negative questions must be used with caution because, if they aren't used carefully, they can make the listener feel he or she is being criticized.

Aren't the Jacksons coming to the New Year's Eve party?	(= I'm surprised that they aren't coming)
Isn't this your old suit?	(= I'm surprised you're not wearing the new one)
Didn't my letter arrive?	(= I'm surprised it hasn't arrived yet)
Won't Timmy spoil his appetite by eating candy before dinner?	(= mild suggestion; = you really *shouldn't* let Timmy eat candy before dinner)
Can't you and your brother play quietly?	(= indirect criticism; = stop being so noisy)
Haven't you finished painting that room yet?	(= criticism/impatience; = you should have finished by now)
Shouldn't you send a "thank-you" note to Aunt Sally?	(= mild suggestion or reminder)
Wasn't your final exam due today?	(= reminder; you *should have* finished your exam by today—have you finished it?)

c. Rhetorical questions and exclamation questions

Rhetorical questions (<u>*Why*</u> *has this happened to me?* <u>*Who*</u> *writes these silly advertisements?* <u>*What kind of*</u> *person does this kind of thing?* <u>*When*</u> *are they going to finish repairing this street,* etc.) are really not questions at all, but a way for the

THE COMPLEX SENTENCE

speaker to express his or her (usually negative) opinions or frustrations in question form. Rhetorical questions allow the speaker to "ask" questions that don't really have any answer (such as philosophical or moral questions), or ones that are so specialized they can't be answered by the average listener. Because of this, it's never necessary to try to answer rhetorical questions since the speaker doesn't really expect any response. Rhetorical questions usually start with a "question word"—usually *why* or *how*, but also *who, what, where,* etc. Because rhetorical questions often show an emotionally stressful mood, there is also verbal stress on the question word.

Another type of emotionally strong statement-question is the exclamation question. Exclamation questions look like negative questions, but we use them in a completely different way. Exclamation questions help the speaker express strong enthusiasm or emotion. The way they differ from rhetorical questions is more than just the form, however. An exclamation question not only includes any listeners, but is really directed at them— even if they seldom answer. Rhetorical questions are a monologue by the speaker; any listeners are just witnesses. Someone using exclamation questions is saying to the listeners, "*This is how I feel—don't you feel the same way*?" Because exclamation questions are very emotional, usually in a positive way, it's easy for the speaker to seem excessively enthusiastic, so use them with caution.

Doesn't **Paula have wonderful skin?**	(= exclamation)
Why **do we think science can answer every need?**	(= rhetorical)
What **ever happened to courtesy?**	(= rhetorical)
What **could Tommy have been thinking of?**	(= rhetorical)
When **is she finally going to be ready?**	(= rhetorical)
Isn't **it a lovely day?**	(= exclamation)
Don't **you adore that color?**	(adore = love very much; = exclamation)
Doesn't **every child get excited at Christmas?**	(= exclamation)
Isn't **Vivaldi's music wonderfully soothing?**	(= exclamation)

170

12 Gerunds and Infinitives

a. Gerunds are not a verb form

We tend to think that if we see a word ending in *-ing* (*eating, sleeping, playing,* etc.), it must be a verb in the progressive tense. That is very often true—all progressive tenses use the verb's *-ing* form (called the *present participle;* the present participle of *walk* is *walking, sleep/sleeping,* etc.). This is by far the most frequent, but not the only use of the present participle. Sometimes that *-ing* is actually one of two other grammar forms. One of these is called a *gerund,* which is a noun made from a verb's present participle, but is not actually a verb at all. In the sentence *I like playing tennis,* what looks like a progressive verb, *playing,* is really a gerund, not the present progressive tense of *play* (the actual verb in the sentence is *like*).

Gerunds have a very important role in English. We use gerunds when we need to make an action the subject or object of a sentence. If we say *I like tennis,* we aren't giving the listener accurate information. What does the speaker *really* like about tennis? Tennis balls? Tennis courts? Tennis shirts? Tennis players? When most people say *I like tennis* (or football, baseball, etc.), they are really saying one of only two things: I like *playing* tennis or I like *watching* tennis.

Because gerunds are nouns, they never indicate tense and never change form in the sentence, regardless of the time frame or number of persons involved. The verb in the sentence changes tense or person when necessary. If the verb that the gerund comes from always has a preposition after it (*talk to, get . . . from, stop at,* etc.), the gerund also uses that preposition (*talking to, getting . . . from, stopping at,* etc.).

There are only two difficulties in using gerunds: when to use them (see section c, *When to use a gerund/when to use an infinitive*), and where to put them in a sentence when we do use them. Gerunds can be used in sentences as either the subject or the object. If they are the subject, they come at the very beginning of a statement (just after the helping verb in a question). If they are the object, they immediately follow the verb.

171

THE COMPLEX SENTENCE

Paul has always enjoyed _writing_ songs.	(= object)
Making words rhyme was easy for him even as a boy.	(= subject)
Naming his songs is the hardest thing for Paul to do.	(= subject)
Singing has never been something Paul does well.	(= subject)
Singers like _performing_ Paul's songs at their concerts.	(= object)
Becoming popular isn't so enjoyable for Paul.	(= subject)
Giving interviews and _talking_ to strangers or _signing_ autographs for them are all especially uncomfortable for him.	(= subject)
He likes _sitting_ in his office and _planning_ his next song.	(= object)

Paul still hates _talking_ to interviewers and _appearing_ on TV talk shows (= object), but _doing_ them has now become part of his career. (= subject of clause following _but_)

b. How gerunds differ from participles

The second nonverb form in English that uses -ing is the present participle either as a *participle-adjective* (*the _speeding_ car, a _frightening_ movie, two _coughing_ children, a roomful of _chattering_ guests, the play is _boring_,* etc.) or, less frequently, as a type of noun phrase (*Ted's _being_ a doctor means he has to work long hours; _Having learned_ Chinese as a child, Mae could translate easily; John, _not wanting_ to disturb the family, decided to go out for breakfast;* etc.—see Chapter 17, section c, *Participles used as nouns and adjectives*).

One way to recognize the difference between a gerund and a present participle used as an adjective is that a participle-adjective always either comes just before a noun and describes (*modifies*) it, just like any other kind of adjective, or comes at the end of the sentence immediately after *be* (. . . *is _irritating_,* . . . *was _amusing_,* . . . *have been _exhausting_,* etc.). In the examples with participle-adjectives, the noun is underlined twice, the participle-adjective once.

Charcoal-grilling is a great way to cook in summer.	(= gerund—subject)
My family really likes _charcoal-grilling_ in summer.	(= gerund—object)
The _charcoal-grilling method_ is a great way to keep the kitchen cool in summer.	(= participle-adjective)
Operating is always the last choice for a good doctor.	(= gerund—subject)
All good doctors avoid _operating_ unless absolutely necessary.	(= gerund—object)
The _operating_ techniques we use today are very safe.	(= participle-adjective)

A participle phrase will sometimes, like a gerund, come at the beginning of a sentence, but only as part of a phrase, not as the entire sentence. Further, in a participle phrase, the helping verb will always be included. The helping verb will be in the -*ing* form, not the full verb. A gerund isn't used this way.

Susan liked _having_ a job in Paris.	(= gerund—object)
Having a job in Paris made Susan happy.	(= gerund—subject)
Susan's _having worked_ in Paris helped her find a new career.	(= participle phrase)
Robin found _being_ single again a frightening, but helpful, experience.	(found = discovered/ learned; = gerund— object)
Being single again gave Robin confidence.	(= gerund—subject)
Being single again, Robin was finally able to become more confident.	(= participle phrase)

THE COMPLEX SENTENCE

I didn't enjoy *realizing* that the children were all grown up and ready to leave home.	(= gerund—object)
Realizing the children were all grown up and ready to leave home has made me feel old.	(= gerund—subject)
Having realized that the children were all grown up and ready to leave home, I began to feel old.	(= participle phrase)

c. When to use a gerund/when to use an infinitive

When you look at examples of gerunds, you may wonder why we don't just use an infinitive (the dictionary form of the verb + *to*: eating →→→ *to eat*; playing →→→ *to play*; etc.). In many sentences, it does seem possible to substitute an infinitive for a gerund.

Getting a taxi at this time of day is impossible. →→→
To get a taxi at this time of day is impossible.

Terry loves *cleaning* the house from top to bottom. →→→
Terry loves *to clean* the house from top to bottom.

Going to the dentist is Richard's worst nightmare. →→→
To go to the dentist is Richard's worst nightmare.

Why can't we then just forget about gerunds and use infinitives all the time? Grammar isn't that simple, but there is a two-part answer to that question. In cases where a gerund is the object of the sentence, it follows the verb. English verbs fall into three groups: verbs of one group must always be followed by a gerund, not an infinitive; verbs of the second group must always be followed by an infinitive, not a gerund; and verbs of the third group can be followed by either an infinitive or a gerund.

These verbs should always be followed by a gerund, not an infinitive:

admit	imagine
appreciate	keep (continue)
avoid	mind (dislike/prefer not to)
complete	postpone
consider	practice
delay	quit
deny	recall
discuss	recommend
dislike	suggest
enjoy	talk
escape	think
finish	understand

These verbs should always be followed by an infinitive, not a gerund:

appear	mean
ask	need
beg	offer
care	persuade
convince	plan
decide	prepare
deserve	pretend
expect	promise
fail	refuse
forget	seem
happen	tend
hope	wait
intend	want
know (how to)	wish
learn (how to)	

THE COMPLEX SENTENCE

These verbs can be followed directly by either an infinitive or a gerund:

afford	love
attempt	neglect
begin	prefer
choose	pretend
come	regret
continue	remember
go	start
hate	stop
hesitate	try
like	

Many of the preceding list of verbs can have quite different meanings, depending on whether they are followed by a gerund or an infinitive. The verb *stop,* especially, has a very limited meaning if it is followed by an infinitive. It then usually means "interrupt action A in order to do action B."

Stop *looking* in the mirror! →→→ . . . stop (walking) (in order) *to look* in a shop window

Stop *trying* to be so tough! →→→ . . . stop (doing something) (in order) *to try* on some clothes

Stop *buying* so many ties! →→→ . . . stop (at the store) (in order) *to* (be able to) *buy* . . .

Stop *taking* my picture! →→→ . . . stop (the bus) (in order) *to take* a picture

The second reason we can't always use infinitives instead of gerunds is that in many cases substituting an infinitive for a gerund can change the meaning quite a bit.

Peter stopped *talking*. (= he became silent)

Peter stopped *to talk* (with someone). (= he stopped walking and began a conversation)

Try *solving* this puzzle. (= see if this puzzle will be enjoyable since other puzzles weren't enjoyable)

Try *to solve* this puzzle. (= attempt to find time or interest in order to solve it)

Remember *mailing* that letter? (= *do you remember* that you mailed it earlier)

Remember *to mail* that letter. (= *don't forget* to mail it later)

Regardless of the verb involved, *only* a gerund can follow a preposition, even if the verb is one that is normally followed only by an infinitive.

forget *to do* →→→→ forget *about doing*

decide *to go* →→→→ decide *on going*

Doug was sorry *about being* late for the meeting.

Doug was sorry *to be* late for the meeting.

Walter and Ruth had planned *on giving* their daughter a big wedding.

Walter and Ruth had planned *to give* their daughter a big wedding.

Morris completely forgot *about buying* wine for the party.

Morris completely forgot *to buy* wine for the party.

Finally, gerunds are always used whenever we talk about recreation, sports, or leisure activities—especially after the verb *come* or *go*.

177

THE COMPLEX SENTENCE

- These "recreational gerunds" are usually used after the verb *come* or *go:*

biking	mountain climbing
bowling	riding/horseback-riding
cycling	sailing
dancing	shopping
diving	sightseeing
drinking	skiing
driving	surfing
fishing	swimming
golfing	walking
hiking	water-skiing
ice skating/figure skating	

- The names of most team sports, games of skill or of chance, etc., are used as part of a gerund phrase after the gerund *playing:*

playing baseball
playing cards
playing checkers
playing chess
playing darts
playing football
playing golf
playing hockey
playing polo
playing roulette
playing soccer
playing tennis
playing volleyball

13 Clauses

Clauses are very important in English because they let us put two shorter ideas together into one longer, more complex sentence. Although there are many kinds of clauses, they all share the same definition: every clause must have a subject and a verb. You have already learned a bit about clauses (see Chapter 10, section b, *Connecting things and thoughts*) and how they differ from phrases, but remember that even though it is part of a longer sentence, a clause can stand on its own and make sense, but a phrase cannot. *When I came home, . . .* is a clause; *every Saturday morning at seven, . . .* is a phrase.

The clause structures in this chapter all contain time expressions, such as *when, before, after*. These sentences include two clauses: the clause with the time word shows the situation (*When I drive to work, . . .*); the other clause (the result clause) usually shows what happens as a result of the situation in the first clause. The idea of the first clause describing the situation and the second clause showing the result will be important later in understanding conditional situations (see Chapter 17, section b, *Conditional forms*).

The second clause can have the same subject and verb as the first clause, or it can have a different subject and verb. One important rule is that both clauses must happen in the same time frame—although the verbs don't always have to have exactly the same tense.

Time Clause	Result Clause
When Tom gets home from the office,	he always reads the paper.
When we got home from Aruba,	Mom picked us up.
Before we make the cake,	we must heat the oven.
After the summer break starts,	I'll look for a job.

THE COMPLEX SENTENCE

a. When

We use *when* clauses to show the general time that something happens, or happened in the past. If we talk about a future event, only the result clause uses *will* or *be going to*. The verb in the time clause uses the simple present. This is also true for *before* and *after*. In written English, the time and result clauses are always separated by a comma.

When Mark *finishes* this book, he*'ll* let you borrow it.

When the painter came, we had to lock up our dog.

When Jane *starts* her new job next month, she*'ll* be able to use a company car.

When the snow melts, the crocuses come out right away.

(crocus = an early spring flower)

For questions, we always add the question word to the result clause, not to the time clause. For negative statements, the negative goes in the usual place after the verb, in either clause.

When Paul *arrives* from Seoul tomorrow, *will* you tell him about your money troubles?

When Ellen called, *what* did she say about her trip to Grenada?

When I *can't* sleep, I drink some warm milk.

When the cats wake me, I do*n't* get angry with them.

The result clause can come in the first position, and the time clause can move to the second position if the sentence will still make sense logically. *We don't use the comma* between the clauses if the result clause comes first.

When the children are at school, it's very quiet in the house.

It's very quiet in the house *when the children are at school*.

b. Before

Before and *after* are used the same way as *when* in time clause structures, but they show the situation that happens before (or after) the situation the result clause talks about.

Before Andrea can be promoted, she will have to take some management courses.

Before we sit down to eat, you had better wash your hands.

We always unplug the toaster before we leave for work.

Before it rains, Uncle Kent's arthritis   (act up = cause trouble) always starts to act up.

Before we can drive to the drugstore, I have to stop at the bank.

c. After

Everything that applies to clauses with *when* and *before* is also true of clauses with *after*.

After you start telling a joke, you always spoil it by laughing.

After I finish my lunch, I'm going to take a nap.

Tom can look for a new apartment after he finds a job.

The roses will start blooming after the weather gets warmer.

After Mary paints the house, she is going to stay with her sister for a few days.

d. Since *(+ noun phrase/simple past)*

Since has a number of different meanings in English. The use of *since* in this case doesn't mean "because"; it means "from the time . . . happened." The time clause event tells what caused the change; the result clause tells what the change was. We often need to use the present perfect when we use *since* in this way.

THE COMPLEX SENTENCE

Since he was fired from his job, Jake has lost all of his confidence.

Since we found a burglar in the living room, I've been scared of being alone.

Since Stephen went on a diet, nobody recognizes him.

Since Jack's death, Eleanor won't see any of her old friends.

The dogs have been so restless since Fred left for the office.

e. If *(vs. When)*

It's sometimes hard to understand the difference between *if* and *when.* We use *when* for situations that the speaker believes are certain—either because they happen regularly, or happened in the past, or because the speaker is very sure they will happen. *If,* on the other hand, tells the listener that one possible (but not probable) situation has to happen *before* a second event can happen. We use *if* to show some doubt about whether something really will happen or not. *If* tells the listener that the event has only a 50 percent likelihood. Sometime, we use *even* before *if.* Such cases show that the speaker is very skeptical about the situation happening.

When Mother comes for a visit, we can give her the sofa in your study to sleep on.	(= 100%)
If Mother comes for a visit, can I give her the sofa in your study to sleep on?	(= 50%)
Even if Mother comes for a visit, we can always get a hotel room for her.	(= 25% or less)
If it starts to snow, may I sleep on your sofa?	(= it may not snow "tonight")
I'm always hesitant to drive *when* it snows.	(= each winter it snows several times)

f. That

When we use certain verbs (such as *think, know, say, tell*) in clauses, we often need to use the word *that* to connect them to the second clause. The second clause usually tells us what the speaker *thinks* or *knows.* Although you can reverse the clauses in time clause structures, in this case the clause with *that* must stay in the first position. The subject of many such *that* clauses is *it* (as in *It seems that* . . . , or *It appears that* . . . , etc.). Some people leave out *that* in informal conversation, but some verbs require it, and it is usually used in many formal or business situations.

The verbs usually or always followed by *that* include:

appear	**say**
decide	**seem**
expect	**suggest**
hope	**tell**
know	**think***
pray	**understand**
regret	
report (= news report, etc.)	

Note: * *Think,* in this case, is never followed by prepositions such as *about, of,* etc. It is only a statement of the speaker's opinion.

The CEO *thinks that* we should expand our sales overseas.

Dad *knows that* his illness is serious.

The paper *says that* we'll have a cold summer.

Barry *tells* me *that* your golf game is improving.

CNN *reports that* 30 people were killed in the recent earthquake.

It *seems that* prices are starting to rise again.

I *understand that* Phil and I went to the same high school, but we never met.

⌊14⌉ Phrasal Verbs

English has a group of two- or three-part verbs called *phrasal verbs*. Each phrasal verb has at least two parts—the verb and another (usually shorter) word. This second word, called the *particle*, is usually, but not always, a preposition like *on, through, over,* etc. Many phrasal verbs in English started as a casual idiomatic expression and with time became an accepted part of everyday language. This makes them "difficult" because the meaning is usually very different from the separate meanings of the verb and particle. For example, *step down* means to "resign from a high position"; *step up* usually means "come forward/come to the front of a public gathering"; neither phrasal verb has much to do with going up or down steps.

There are two basic types of phrasal verbs: separable and inseparable. Inseparable phrasal verbs may consist of two or three words. Separable phrasal verbs are always two words and always have an object. The object can come between the verb and the particle (if it's an object pronoun such as *him, them,* etc., it *must* come between the two parts), or it can come after the particle.

---

think over = to evaluate; to consider before deciding

correct:	**think over *the proposal***
correct:	**think *the proposal* over**
correct:	**think *it* over**
incorrect:	**think over *it***

Inseparable phrasal verbs are exactly that: they cannot be separated. Some of these inseparable phrasal verbs have objects, but they always come *after* the sentence's phrasal verb, never between the verb and particle. Many two-word phrasal verbs, and all three-word phrasal verbs, belong to this group. Some inseparable phrasal verbs do not take an object.

Remember these important characteristics of phrasal verbs:

- with phrasal verbs, the verb always comes before the particle, never after

- the meaning is not necessarily similar to, even more rarely the same as, the basic verb that the phrasal verb originated from

- changing the particle—the second (second *and* third in the case of three-word phrasal verbs), usually smaller, part of the phrasal verb—will change the meaning of any phrasal verb *completely*

- phrasal verbs have all the different tenses that ordinary verbs do, and must agree in tense with the time frame of the sentence

- the position of the object—if there is one—of a phrasal verb depends on whether or not the phrasal verb is separable or inseparable

- most phrasal verbs are completely idiomatic—their real meanings have no logic (the phrasal verb *figure out* doesn't mean "to gain weight" or "to wear revealing clothing"; it means "to solve a problem or mystery through logical steps")

- many phrasal verbs can have both separable and inseparable forms; there can be at least two different meanings—sometimes several—depending on whether you are using the separable or inseparable form of a particular phrasal verb

The sedative *calmed* the patient *down*.	(= made him or her quiet—separable)
Bob *calmed down* after a long walk.	(= stopped being upset—inseparable)
The professor *broke* the formula *down*.	(= divided into steps, segments, or sections; simplified—separable)
This computer has *broken down* twice this month.	(= computer stopped working—inseparable)
Anna *broke down* completely during the funeral.	(= started crying uncontrollably—inseparable)
Sarah *looked* the bank's number *up*.	(= found in phone book—separable)
We all *looked up* when Adam dropped his plate.	(= raised our eyes—inseparable)

THE COMPLEX SENTENCE

The following examples show how much the meanings of phrasal verbs can change with a different particle:

to sit	position the body on a chair, sofa, or seat
to sit down	change from a standing to a sitting position
to sit up	change position of the upper body from lying flat; straighten the back while sitting
to sit through	wait until an (often boring) event ends before leaving
to sit by	remain a passive spectator when action is needed
to sit for	take a major scholastic exam (*mainly British*); have a professional portrait done or photograph taken
to sit around	sit casually and without purpose
to sit in	protest passively by sitting in a forbidden area
to sit in for someone	be somewhere in place of the person who can't be there
to sit in on	attend a meeting or lecture without participating

Finally, to avoid confusion, it's important to remember that English has many traditional verb–preposition combinations that may sound like phrasal verbs but are not.* Here are some:

agree on/with	belong to
apologize for	care about/for
approve of	complain to
argue about/over/with	consist of
believe in	decide on

depend (up)on	search for
die from	suffer from
hear about/from/of	talk about/to/with
laugh about/at	think about/of
listen for/to	wait for
look after/around/at	work for/with
pay for	

Note: *Many of these verbs are part of a phrasal verb combination *if* they are followed by a different preposition. Even though *look at* is just a verb–preposition combination, *look over, look through, look up, look like,* and *look out* (*for*) are all phrasal verbs.

a. Separable phrasal verbs with an object

With these phrasal verbs, the verb and particle can be separated by an object. A separable phrasal verb doesn't *have to* be separated (except if the object is a pronoun—then it must go between the verb and particle). Every *separable* phrasal verb can take an object.

Anne *brought <u>her children</u> up* very well.

Michael! Do you want to *check out <u>the new movie at the mall</u>*?

Joe and Tina's new house has a structural problem, but they didn't *find <u>that</u> out* until after they moved in.

Susie's mother is trying to *turn <u>her</u> into* a professional singer.

Let's *call <u>the wedding</u> off* if that's how you feel!

Here are some separable phrasal verbs. Verbs marked with an asterisk (*) have an identical, but inseparable, form with a different meaning.

*add up	find the total amount of several figures

THE COMPLEX SENTENCE

back up	move a car in reverse; return to an earlier part of a discussion
bring out	show (usually to advantage); expose (flaw or weakness)
bring up	raise children; introduce a new subject in conversation
bring/take back	return something to a shop, etc.
call off	cancel plans
*calm down	soothe *another* person who is upset
*check out	investigate
*fill in/out	write information on a form
find out	discover information
give back	return something to a person
*look up	check facts in a dictionary, etc.
pick out	choose from among several items
pick up	lift from the floor; stop a car and get a person/thing
put away	return something to its proper place
put in	add or insert
put off	postpone something; offend someone
put on	add an article of clothing to the body
show off	display object or skill with pride
*take off	remove an article of clothing from the body
take/pull out	remove
think over	carefully review an opinion/decision
try on	put on clothing to check for style, size, etc.
turn down	lower volume on TV, etc./reject an offer or request
*turn into	make another person/situation change
work out	solve a problem/reach a compromise

b. Inseparable phrasal verbs with an object

These phrasal verbs can never be separated by an object. Although the verb and particle must stay together, they are followed by an object. *All* three-word phrasal verbs belong to this group.

I know that you *cared for* your father better than any nurse.

Please *look after* the dogs.

Don't *ever hang up on* me again!

Terry knows that his wife is the only person who will *put up with* him.

Mary *ran across* the road to find her dog.

Here are some inseparable two-word phrasal verbs *with* an object. Verbs marked with an asterisk (*) have an identical form with a different meaning.

call on	**visit someone**
care for	**be fond of someone; take care of someone**
check into	**register at a hotel; research a subject**
count on	**rely on someone to do something**
go on	**continue** (often followed by a gerund)
go over	**reexamine; review**
go through	**use something up; go over in sequence; endure**
go up	**rising (often for prices or temperatures)**
hang up	**put the phone receiver back**
look after	**take care of someone or something**
look into	**investigate a situation or a person**
run across	**accidentally find something**
run into	**accidentally meet someone**
*turn into	**a person/situation becomes different**

THE COMPLEX SENTENCE

These inseparable three-word phrasal verbs all take an object:

break up with	**end a relationship** (usually people, but also businesses)
call out to	**shout to get someone's attention**
check out of	**pay the bill on leaving a hotel, hospital, etc.**
get along with	**have friendly/smooth relations with**
get on with	**start doing something** (after hesitating, postponing)
get out of	**leave a small vehicle** (car, elevator, etc.)
get rid of	**throw something out/persuade a person to leave**
go along with	**agree with someone/something**
keep up with	**maintain the current speed or level**
look forward to	**anticipate an enjoyable future event**
put up with	**endure an unpleasant situation/behavior**
run out of	**the supply of something ends**
stand up to	**resist someone or some force**

c. Phrasal verbs without an object

These phrasal verbs can never be separated and can never have an object. Anything that follows the phrasal verb is something other than an object. These phrasal verbs are often put at the end of the sentence.

Most men never *grow up*.
We can't cook, so we *eat out* very often.
I usually *wake up* at 5:00 a.m.
My plane *takes off* in a couple of hours.
We often had only a few dollars, but we always *got by*.

Here are some inseparable two-word phrasal verbs with *no* object. Verbs marked with an asterisk (*) have an identical form with a different meaning.

act up	a person behaves badly
*add up	something lacks logic (negative sense)
*break down	a mechanism or machine stops working
*calm down	person returns to calm by himself/herself
come/go back	return to a place
come/go in(to)	enter a place (building, etc.)
eat in	eat at home
eat out	go to restaurants (vs. "eat in")
*fill in/fill in for	substitute for someone else
get by	manage in a difficult situation
get up	leave one's bed and stand up
give in	stop resisting
*give up	lose hope
go out	leave a place
grow up	become an adult
*keep on	continue
*look up	raise eyes
sit down	change from a standing to sitting position
stand up	rise to a standing position
*take off	a plane leaves
*wake up	open one's eyes after sleeping
*work out	do exercise (at a gym)

Relative Clauses

a. Types of clauses

Of all the clause structures in English, relative clauses are the most important. Before discussing relative clauses in detail, some general features of clauses need to be made clear.

A clause is used as part of a larger sentence. That sentence often consists of two clauses, usually of different types. There are two general types of clauses, *independent* and *dependent*. Independent clauses can stand on their own as complete sentences. On the other hand, dependent clauses' meanings are incomplete if we take them out of the sentences they are used in—they need the independent clause, or some other part of the sentence, to explain their meaning. This is the reason they are called *dependent* clauses.

In a relative clause structure, the first clause is an independent clause. This is followed by a *relative pronoun* that introduces the second clause, sometimes a dependent clause, but sometimes an independent clause as well. In a relative clause sentence, the clause that follows the relative pronoun is the *relative clause,* whereas the first clause, the independent clause, is the *main clause*. Unlike time clauses (see Chapter 13), the main and relative clauses *cannot* be reversed. The relative clause must always come in the second position. Additionally, the relative clause always comes after the relative pronoun, *never* before it.

A relative clause always gives a specific piece of information about *something* in the main clause. The relative pronoun is like an arrow pointing back at the main clause, telling us what word the relative clause is describing.

These are the most common relative pronouns:

that	for essential relative clauses referring to nonhuman subjects

which	for nonessential relative clauses referring to nonhuman subjects
who	for both essential and nonessential clauses about people or named animal subjects
whose*	for something or someone "owned" by a person
of which*	for something "owned" by a group or another "thing," such as a building, corporation, etc.

Here are some relative clauses and the way they are formed:

My mother lives in Paris. _She_ is a wonderful cook. →→→
My mother, _who_ lives in Paris, is a wonderful cook.

A young couple live next door. _They_ are from Wisconsin.
→→→ A young couple _who_ live next door are from Wisconsin.

You gave me a book. _It_ got wet. →→→ The book _that_ you gave me got wet.

Tammy has several dolls. The blonde one was stolen. _It_ was Tammy's favorite. →→→ The blonde doll, _which_ was Tammy's favorite, was stolen.

Tina is my eldest daughter. _Her_ name is not a contraction of Christina. →→→ Tina, _whose_ name is not a contraction of Christina, is my eldest daughter.

Mother gave me a set of 10 dinner plates. My husband broke _one of them_. →→→ Mother gave me a set of 10 dinner plates, _one of which_ my husband broke.

Note: *If the "owner" is a person or animal (or other _living_ thing except for plants), we use _whose_ as the relative pronoun. If the "owner" is an object or other thing, or if we're speaking about a general category of living thing instead of a specific one, we use _of which_ as the relative pronoun.

In some of the preceding examples, the relative clause comes in the middle of the main clause instead of after, and we use a comma before and after it to separate it from the main clause.

THE COMPLEX SENTENCE

This is a very important point. Some relative clauses give information about the main clause that is essential to the meaning of the sentence. Other relative clauses give additional, but not so important, information about the main clause. We don't *really* need it to understand the meaning of the sentence. If we remove it, we can still understand the main clause.

When a relative clause gives important information, we call it an *essential clause*—we must have it in order to understand the important point of the main clause. When the information is just a secondary comment—like spoken parentheses, and it doesn't contain essential information—we call it a *nonessential* clause.

In American English, we use the relative pronoun *that* (for things or unnamed animals, etc.) to introduce an essential clause, and we never separate it from the main clause with a comma. We use the relative pronoun *which* (also for things or unnamed animals, etc.) to introduce a nonessential clause, and we *always* separate it from the main clause with a comma if the nonessential clause comes at the end of the sentence, or a pair of commas when it comes in the middle of the sentence.

We use the relative pronoun *who* (for people or *named* animals) to introduce both essential and nonessential clauses, but we still set the nonessential clause apart from the main clause by a pair of commas. It takes some practice, even for native speakers, to know whether a relative clause is essential or nonessential. Here are some more examples showing how to use *that* or *which*:

This dress is the one _that_ Elizabeth Taylor wore in *Cleopatra.*	(= we have to know why the dress is special)
This dress, _which_ is the one Elizabeth Taylor wore in *Cleopatra,* **cost $10,000 in 1963.**	(= the price of the dress is important, not who wore it or what film it was in)
The Lobster Trap is a restaurant *that* **specializes in excellent lobster dishes.**	(= we have to know what makes the restaurant special)
The Lobster Trap, _which_ is a seafood restaurant, is one of the best places in the city.	(= the quality of the restaurant is more important than the kind of food)

Soignée is a French word *that* means "elegant."	(= the meaning of the word is very important to the speaker)
Soignée, *which* is a French word for "elegant," is most often used about fashion and décor.	(= how the word is used is more important to the speaker than its meaning)

b. That

The first car *that* Hal bought after he got his license in 1979 was a Mustang.

The old slippers *that* Jane threw out last month were very comfortable.

In the attic, I saw a cookbook *that* my kids had given me and brought it downstairs.

Dad doesn't know why the dog *that* lives next door keeps barking at him.

c. Which

Chris's dogs, *which* Helen never wanted, have ruined Helen's new rug.

The story in yesterday's paper, *which* I never had time to read, was about a friend of mine.

The wildflowers, *which* are all in bloom now, are making Jan's allergies act up.

The house on the corner, *which* I really wanted to buy, was sold yesterday.

Rouille, *which* is a very spicy mayonnaise, is served with bouillabaisse in Marseilles.

d. Who

The first example of each pair of sentences is an essential clause; the second is a nonessential clause.

> Michael Zane is the man _who_ owns the company where my father works.
>
> Michael Zane, _who_ owns the company where my father works, lives in a small house.
>
> The drunken driver _who_ ran Harriet's father over was arrested last week.
>
> The drunken driver, _who_ ran Harriet's father over, is responsible for a total of six hit-and-run accidents.
>
> Senator Thornton is a man _who_ my husband went to school with.*
>
> Wally Thornton, with _whom_ my husband went to school, is now a senator.*

Note: *In formal written English, if the person the relative clause is talking about is the object, the relative pronoun is _whom_ instead of _who_. Few people nowadays, especially in the United States, use this form in spoken English.

e. Whose/of which

In the following examples, the "owner" is underlined twice, and the relative pronoun(s) once.

> Granddad's <u>will</u>, the details _of which_ are unknown, is going to be read by his lawyer.
>
> <u>My Aunt Maggie</u>, _whose_ vision was failing, has just had laser eye surgery _that_ restored her vision.
>
> <u>That gray house</u> over there, the ground floor _of which_ was built in 1680, was just bought by a historical trust.

16 Quoting Others; Reported Speech

a. Quoting directly

We often have to tell another person what someone else said. English has two ways to do that. The first of these is direct quotation. With direct quotation, we use the person's words exactly as he or she said them.

The second way is to put the other person's words into our own sentence. This is usually called reported speech because the speaker is "reporting" the words of another person to the listener. The way we form reported speech is very logical and consistent, but we need to change the tense of the original speaker's words, and any time expressions.

The two verbs we use most often, either when quoting or when giving reported speech, are *say* and *tell*. These verbs are not interchangeable because they answer different questions.

What did he *say*? →→→ He said, "*I'm going to bed.*"

Who did he *tell*? →→→ He told *me*.

Say emphasizes the information; *tell* emphasizes the person who got the information and has to be used with an object pronoun such as *me, him, them,* etc.

Direct quotations are easy because you just repeat the original speaker's words *exactly.* Be careful not to use the word *that* because it signals reported speech instead of a direct quotation.

| original words: | **"The water is boiling."** |
| direct quotation: | **She said, "The water is boiling."** |

197

original words:	"Who's there?"
direct quotation:	He asked, "Who's there?"

b. Reported speech

Reported speech is a little more complicated for two reasons: there must be a change in tense, and a time expression such as *today* has to change because the "today" of the original speaker, and the "today" of the listener, are usually different days. Be sure to add *that* because you're setting the quotation off from your own words with it.

original words:	"I *am* tired."
reported speech:	He said that he *was* tired.
original words:	"We *are* going to drive."
reported speech:	They said that they *were* going to drive.
original words:	"I'll *be* there."
reported speech:	She said that she *would be* there.
original words:	"He *has been* in France this week."
reported speech:	They told me that he *had been* in France that week.
original words:	"I *was reading* the paper when the tornado hit."
reported speech:	He said that he *had been reading* the paper when the tornado hit.

Don't forget to change any time expressions that may be part of the quotation.

Direct Speech	Reported Speech
now	then (at that time)
today	that day
tonight	that night
tomorrow	the next day (the following day)
yesterday	the previous day/the day before
this week/morning	that week/that morning
last week/month, etc.	the previous . . . /the preceding . . .
next week/month, etc.	the following . . . /the next . . .

Advanced Grammar Forms

a. The passive voice

In the usual English sentence, the subject does something that the verb describes. This is an *active* sentence. Another very important type of sentence is the passive sentence, where the verb takes the lead. Instead of *doing* something actively, the subject is passive and something *is done* to it—the subject receives the effect of the action instead of doing something to the object.

This passive form says to the listener or reader, "the effect of action on me is more important than the action itself." We use *be* as a helping verb together with the verb's past participle (*be done, are made, was spoken, has been broken,* etc.) for all passive voice sentences. Since the passive voice isn't a tense, *be* changes tense to show the different time frames.

to be done

is done

is being done

was done

was being done

will be done

is going to be done

has been done

had been done

will have been done

All modals and helping verbs can also be used in the passive voice.

can be done
could be done
had better be done
has to be done
may be done
might be done
must be done
ought to be done
should be done
would be done

Active	Passive
do	be done
drive	be driven
eat	be eaten
make	be made
send	be sent
speak	be spoken
take	be taken
use	be used
watch	be watched

There is a definite time to use the passive voice and a time to use an active sentence. Following is when to use the passive voice:

- when the way the subject received an action is more important than the person or situation that caused it

The hit-and-run victim *was found* by the side of the road.
(we don't say . . . the police found a hit-and-run victim . . . because the victim is more important than the people who discovered the accident)

My favorite watch *was stolen* last week.

Our son *was born* during our 1992 trip to India.

The mugger *was arrested* when his car ran out of gas on the highway.

Our flight to Paris *was canceled* without explanation.

Many jobs *were lost* when my husband's company declared bankruptcy.

If we want to name the person or thing that did the action (the *agent*), we set it off at the end of the passive sentence with *by*:

The book was written <u>by</u> Tolstoy.

This photo was taken <u>by</u> my mother.

Our fundraiser is going to be attended <u>by</u> many people.

- when we give facts or background information about something

The right-of-survivorship law *has been in effect* for several years.

The world's most famous blue diamond *was donated* to the Smithsonian Institution after the owner's death.

Although the smallpox virus *has been eradicated,* a drug-resistant strain of tuberculosis *has been identified*.

- when we know the result of the action, but not who or what caused it

Despite many theories, no clue to the killer's identity *was* ever *discovered*.

The origin of the disease *is* still *being debated*.

Broken glass *was found* at the location.

- when we already know who did the action, and we want to focus on what happened

Willy's shirts *were pressed* with an iron that was much too hot.
Sally *has been stopped* twice for traffic violations.
Bob and Christina's house *is being renovated*.

- when the speaker wants to sound impersonal or objective, such as with a news report, notices, and signs

Traffic *has been rerouted* to avoid the scene of the accident.
This establishment *has been closed* by order of the health commissioner.
Shoplifters *will be prosecuted*.

- when evaluating success or failure, or when judging quality

The turkey *was overcooked*.
None of the knives *had been* properly *sharpened*.
Violations of the health code *have been discovered*.

Remember that we can use the passive voice only with transitive verbs (verbs that take an object), never with intransitive verbs:

The earthquake occurred on a Sunday. →→→ Many houses *were damaged*.
Terry slept until 9:00. →→→ The bed *was made* with linen sheets.
Our cats meowed all night. →→→ The neighbors *were awakened* by the noise.

THE COMPLEX SENTENCE

Sometimes in casual conversations, *get* is substituted for *be* in passive sentences.

Perry's foot *got cut* on some glass at the beach.
The house next door *got broken into* last night.
Sarah *got fired* yesterday.

Following is when *not* to use the passive voice:

- when the natural focus is on who did the action

Bart built a fire.
Bill won the match and the tournament.
The president held a press conference.

b. Conditional forms

All conditional sentences have two clauses, each describing a situation. One of the situations must exist for the second situation to happen. One of the clauses always has the word *if* (or a similar word) in it. This clause, called the *if clause*, describes the degree of possibility (how likely or unlikely the situation is). The other clause explains the impossible, unlikely, possible, or very likely result, and is called *the result clause*.

if clause:	**If the shops are still open after work,**
result:	**I can do some shopping.**
if clause:	**If the shops are already closed,**
result:	**I'll have to go shopping on Saturday.**

In addition to the simple *if* clauses introduced in Chapter 13, section e, there are three main conditionals: the future conditional, the "unreal" conditional, and the past conditional. Each conditional form has a strict word order, although like all "equal" clauses, you can usually reverse the clauses and keep the meaning. Nevertheless, most conditionals start with the *if* clause, followed by the result clause. It's important to understand each conditional form and how it is used because the different forms have very definite uses.

- Future conditional

In the future conditional, the *if* clause is followed by the simple present tense of the verb (*go, take, say,* etc.), and the result clause has *will* and the simple form of the verb.

The future conditional describes a possible situation in the immediate or distant future.

If the rain *continues,* all the vegetables *will* die.

If Patricia *makes* one more comment about my gray hair, I'*ll* leave!

I'*ll* go to the party *if* I *can leave* the office early.

Douglas *will buy* a new house *if* interest rates *stay* low.

What *will* you *do* if the company *closes*?

- Unreal conditional

In the unreal conditional, the *if* clause is followed by the *simple past tense* of the verb (*went, took, said,* etc.), or if the verb is *be,* we use *were,* not *was, for all persons,* and the result clause has *would, could,* or *might,* and the simple form of the verb.

The unreal conditional describes an unreal or nearly impossible situation, and is used when we talk about unlikely or impossible hopes or wishes.

If you *were* rich, what *would* you *buy* first?

If Sam *were promoted,* we *would* all *be fired.*

If I *spoke* French, I *could study* at the Sorbonne.

If I *were* younger, I would *sail* around the world.

I *might be able to* give the boss some advice, *if* he *would listen* to me.

THE COMPLEX SENTENCE

• Past conditional

In the past conditional, the *if* clause is followed by *had* as a helping verb and the *past participle* of the verb (*had gone, had taken, had said,* etc.), or if the verb is *be, had been.* The result clause has *would have, could have, should have,* or *might have,* and the past participle of the verb (*done, spoken, made*).

The past conditional speculates on *past* events—what "*. . . would have happened if I hadn't done this . . . ,*" etc.

Aunt Hilda *might have found* a husband *if she hadn't worked* so hard all her life.

Would you *have been* happier *if* the university *hadn't given* you that scholarship?

You *wouldn't be* so sure of yourself *if* you *had seen* as much of life as I had at your age.

c. Participles used as adjectives and phrases

Each English verb has two participle forms, the present and past participles. Participles are verb forms, not tenses, but they are used to construct many tenses, and they have other important language functions as well.

The present participle always ends in *–ing* (*run →→→ running*; *write →→→ writing,* etc.). The past participle of regular verbs ends in *–ed,* just like the simple past tense, but the past participle of irregular verbs varies (*cut →→→ cut; break →→→ broken; get →→→ gotten;* etc.). It's the past participle, together with the helping verb, *have,* that we use to construct the present perfect tense.

Participles are used for many things other than tenses, however. They are often used as adjectives or nouns. Both past and present participles are used as adjectives, but their uses and meanings are quite different and are often confused. One way to keep the two types apart is that past participle adjectives are often followed by prepositions linking them to the rest of the sentence, whereas present participle adjectives usually come at or very near the end of the sentence.

Present Participle Adjectives	Past Participle Adjectives
(is) amusing	(is) amused *by* . . .
(is) boring	(is) bored *by* . . .
(is) disgusting	(is) disgusted *by/with* . . .
(is) exciting	(is) excited *by/about* . . .
(is) interesting	(is) interested *in* . . .
(is) tiring	(is) tired *of* . . .
(is) surprising	(is) surprised *by* . . .
(is) irritating	(is) irritated *by* . . .
(is) worrying	(is) worried *by/about* . . .
(is) disappointing	(is) disappointed *by/in* . . .
(is) embarrassing	(is) embarrassed *by* . . .

Although these adjectives often follow the verb *be,* they can also follow *state-of-being* verbs (see Chapter 2, section b, *Types of verbs*).

If we substitute one of these adjective types for the other, the meaning of the sentence changes completely. *Past* participle adjectives always describe the subject's <u>reaction</u>, or the <u>effect</u> on the speaker. *Present* participle adjectives, on the other hand, describe the essential character of the subject.

I'm always *amused* by Steve's stories.	(= the stories' *effect* on the speaker)
Steve's stories are always so *amusing*.	(= the fundamental character of the stories)
I'm so *bored* by these speeches!	(= the speeches' *effect* on the speaker)
Henderson's speech is so *boring*!	(= the true quality of the speech)
Joey, I'm *disgusted* with your behavior.	(= the speaker's *reaction* to Joey's behavior)
Joey, your behavior is *disgusting*!	(= the actual nature of Joey's behavior)

THE COMPLEX SENTENCE

Cynthia is _interested_ in Etruscan art.	(= the _effect_ of Etruscan art on her)
Cynthia thinks Etruscan art _is_ an _interesting_ subject.	(= the fundamental quality of Etruscan art, in Cynthia's opinion)

A final word about participles used as adjectives: don't confuse present participle adjectives with gerunds (see Chapter 12).

Participle phrases are another major way in which present participles are used in English sentences. They can appear at the beginning of a sentence, introducing the subject like a giant adjective. They can also come in the middle of the sentence, between the subject and the verb, as a comment (a kind of spoken parentheses) outside the action of the sentence. In the following examples, the subject that the participle phrase is describing is underlined.

Not having been washed for generations, **the house's** many **windows** let in hardly any light.

Working until dawn, **Harry** finally finished the last chapter of his book.

The **store**, _having stood empty since the previous year,_ has now been rented.

Wanting security, **Grace** married a man she didn't really love.

d. Reflexive pronouns

Reflexive pronouns are used when the action of the subject isn't directed at another person or thing, but back to the subject. Reflexive pronouns for all singular subjects end in _–self_; those for all plural subjects end in _–selves_.

Betty looks at Susan. →→→ **Betty looks at _her_.**
Betty looks at Betty. →→→ **Betty looks at _herself_.**

Betty and Susan look at Joey and Ted. →→→ **Betty and Susan look at _them_.**

Betty and Susan look at Betty and Susan. →→→ Betty and Susan look at *them<u>selves</u>*.

These are the reflexives used in English:

I →→→ **myself**
you →→→ **yourself***
he →→→ **himself**
she →→→ **herself**
it →→→ **itself**
we →→→ **ourselves**
they →→→ **themselves**

Note: *If *you* is used to mean "you two," etc., the reflexive has to be plural, *your<u>selves</u>*.

Reflexive pronouns are used only when the subject directs the action at himself or herself. Any other use is incorrect. Some speakers, unsure of whether to use the subject or object pronoun in certain cases, will use a reflexive pronoun instead of the correct pronoun just to avoid making the choice between *I* and *me*.

correct:	**I received a letter for my wife and me.**
	(it was for my wife and it was *for me*)
<u>incorrect</u>:	**I received a letter for my wife and I.**
<u>incorrect</u>:	**I received a letter for my wife and myself.**

English uses reflexive pronouns far less than most other Western languages and only in cases like these:

Did you *<u>enjoy</u> yourselves* at the movies, boys?
Ow! I just *<u>cut</u> myself* on this bottle.

209

THE COMPLEX SENTENCE

Paul *looked at* himself after his haircut and was not pleased.

Our new neighbors *introduced* themselves to me when I took in the morning paper.

Daddy's *making a fool of* himself over that pretty nurse!

In addition to the verbs used in the preceding examples, here are a few other verbs that are often or usually used with reflexive pronouns:

examine

wash

shave

blame

criticize

be proud of

hurt

take care of

tell

teach

scold

make –self sick

pity/feel sorry for

Finally, an important distinction is whether or not to use *by* with a reflexive pronoun. Generally, *by myself* means "alone," whereas *myself* simply means "I did it without help."

I'd like to sit over there *by myself* for a little while.

Janet painted the kitchen *herself.*

Joe and Sally want to be *by themselves.*

Do you want some help, or can you manage it *yourself*?

ADVANCED GRAMMAR FORMS

e. Causative and permissive verbs

We don't always do things ourselves. Sometimes we ask someone else to do something for us. For those situations, English has a form, called *causatives,* that shows how one person "asks" another person to do something.

Similar to causatives is another group of verbs called *permissives.* The difference is that with causatives, the person doing the action is neutral, but the other person wants it done. With permissives, the person doing the action actually wants to do it, while the first person gives him or her "permission."

There are two causative forms. In the first form (1), the task or service is more important than the person doing it; in the second form (2), the person who does the service is more important. Some causatives can be used with either form, but others (as well as all permissives) can be used only in the second form. The first form uses the main verb's *past participle (I had my car's oil* checked*);* the second form uses the main verb's infinitive or simple form* *(I had my sister* bring *me back a bottle of wine from her trip to France).*

Note: *Some verbs in the second form need *to* before the verb, others don't.

Susan let the baby *have* another cookie.

Susan allowed the baby *to have* another cookie.

The word order in causative sentences cannot be changed. It must follow the exact pattern. Here are the most common causative and permissive forms.

Causatives

have something *done* (1)

get something *done* (1)

have someone *do* something (2)

make someone *do* something (2)

THE COMPLEX SENTENCE

Permissives

let someone *do* something (2)

allow someone *to do* something (2)

permit someone *to do* something (2)

help someone *to do* something (2)

encourage someone *to do* something (2)

Have is the most widely used of any verb for causatives. With all verbs in causative sentences, almost any tense can be used.

I *had* my car *repaired* by the mechanic.

The neighbors *are having* an air-conditioner *installed.*

We *are going to have* our windows *washed* next week.

Until recently, my father *has had* all his business letters *written* by his secretary.

In the second form, the person doing the action comes between the helping verb and the main verb.

Meg usually *has* her son *wash the car* each Saturday morning.

Our boss *has been having* us *help* him with the annual report.

I usually *have* my doctor *take* a chest x-ray every six months.

18 Words Used in Many Ways

English has certain words that are used in many expressions and have a wide variety of meanings. Some of these are idiomatic expressions or verb–object combinations, but very few are phrasal verbs. Learning these different meanings is one of the best ways to increase vocabulary.

a. The uses of have

The verb *have* is used in these ways:

- as a helping verb in all the perfect tenses

I *have* already *eaten.*
He *had spoken* to the boss by the time I got to the office.
They *will have driven* 75 miles before they see the first gas station.

- as a modal meaning "obligation"

Tell Maurice that he *has to* attend the meeting.

- as a modal meaning "you should . . . "

The doctors told Mother she *had better do* more exercise.

- as the helping verb in most causative sentences (see Chapter 17, section e)

We've *had* the beach house *painted* twice in the last three years.

Mrs. Rosen always *has* the dry cleaner *deliver* her clothing.

- as an imperative meaning "be/behave *this* way"

Have some consideration—I've had such a difficult day!

Have a bit of compassion—Larry's son is in the hospital!

- as part of many expressions, verb–preposition combinations, and some phrasal verbs

Don *has* a lot of money. (to own, possess, etc.)

They *have* two cars and a lovely home.

We *have* a large family. (be connected to)

Aunt Karen and Uncle Steve *never had* children. (produce children)

Have another slice of roast beef, Arthur! (take)

What did you *have for dinner*? (eat)

The Logans *had* a terrible car *accident*.

The morning news said that they'*d had* a big *earthquake* in Japan.

He said he *was having pain* in his lower back.

I really do *have a headache*. (or other "–aches," a cold, the flu, etc.)

We don't *have time for* this now.

I *have had it with* you, Joey! (cannot endure any more of a bad situation)

Have fun at the baseball game, boys! (enjoy)

Did you *have a good time* in Jamaica, Carol? (enjoyable experiences)

I *have an idea*—let's *have champagne* with dinner!

Have a heart, Ben! Let the dog come in out of the snow!
(be kind)

It *has to do with* fairness, not money. (it concerns; the subject is)

Have a look at this report, Sam. (look carefully; examine)

We've been *having* a cool summer this year.

I think you should *have* some more *patience* with the children.

b. *The uses of* take

> *Take* is another verb that is used in a great many expressions. Aside from the usual meaning of "pick up," we use *take* in these expressions:

I'll need to *take* some time *off* next week.	(= be away from his or her job)
Let's *take* a few sandwiches along with us on the drive.	
Take a break and go for a short walk.	(= interrupt task briefly to relax)
When the CEO *took charge* of this company, business was terrible.	(= began his job)
Anne *takes* two showers a day.	
Do you *take* me *for* an idiot?	(= do you think I'm stupid?)
He's always *taken on* too much responsibility.	(= accept tasks)
Please *take the time* to do this job thoroughly.	(= don't rush)
Take this medicine one hour before meals.	(= swallow)
It should *take effect* within a few hours or less.	(= medicine begins to work)
Could you *take a look* at these sales figures?	(= please examine and give your opinion)
I'm going to *take a nap* for an hour or so.	(nap = short sleep at unusual time)

Take care!	(= be careful)
Could you *take care of* my dog while I'm away?	(= look after)
My father *takes advantage of* every tax break.	(= use for one's own benefit)
I have to *take* the car in to be serviced.	(= bring it to the garage)
They asked me to *take* their picture at the zoo.	(= photograph)
Take a seat, I'll be right with you.	(= sit down)
The new manager will *take over* next month.	(= one person leaves a job; another person takes over the same job)
Be sure to *take hold* of my hand when we get on the escalator.	(= grasp)
Al doesn't even *take the trouble* to thank his wife for the meals she cooks for him.	(= make an effort)
Mother always *takes pains* to set a beautiful table for meals.	(= makes a big effort)
I'd prefer to *take* the train.	(= ride)
He *took* the news very calmly.	(= react to an unexpected event)

c. *The uses of* get

Get is probably used in more ways than any other English verb, with the possible exceptions of *do* and *make.* A lot of these expressions use *get* to mean *become (get tired),* but it can also mean *receive, find, reach a destination,* or *change condition or situation.* Some idiomatic expressions with *have . . . got (Have you got time for a drink; Have you got any coins on you?)* or *have got to (I've got to go to the bank this afternoon)* are really another way of using *have, have to,* or *must.*

We use *get* in casual speech or conversational English together with the past participle of the main verb to form certain causative sentences, or as a casual form of the passive voice (see Chapter 17, sections e and a, respectively).

These reports must *get done* by 5:00. (be finished)

Teddy *got scolded* by his mother. (was scolded)

Anita *got* badly *cut* by flying glass when her car crashed.
(was cut)

The boss wants you to *get* these packages *sent out* today.
(have them sent)

We really must *get* the house *cleaned* and *get* the windows
washed. (have someone clean the house/wash the windows, etc.)

We also use *get* in these expressions:

Bill has gone to the store to *get* some milk.	(= find and buy)
Let's *get* going!	(= leave; go out; start doing)
Just when Brian was starting to *get ahead,* he lost his job.	(= make success/progress; save money)
I couldn't *get to* the last three reports today.	(= find enough time to do/read/write, etc.)
If we don't leave now, we won't be able to *get to* the station in time.	(= reach; arrive)
Tom's flight should *have gotten to* Paris by now.	(= arrived in)
Give me a few minutes to *get dressed.*	(= put on clothes)
Mary *gets tired* so easily nowadays.	(= feel the need to rest)
Get away from me!	(= Leave . . . alone! Go away!)
A few more meals like this and I'm going to *get fat.*	(= become fat)
This is a complicated joke—tell me if you don't *get it.*	("get it" = slang for "understand")
You must *have gotten it wrong*— that's not the correct procedure at all.	(get it wrong = misunderstand; do . . . incorrectly)
My little dog is starting to *get on* in years.	(= reaching an advanced age)

Oh, *get on* with it! (= finish doing; stop hesitating and do . . .)

You really should *get* (some) *sleep.* (=go to sleep for a while)

This room is too warm—I'm *getting sleepy.* (= become physically sleepy)

Dad is planning to *get together with* his fellow golfers this Sunday. (= agree to meet)

Are you going to *get up* now? (= stand up from bed)

This June, we'll *get* a pay *raise/ promotion.* (= be given a higher salary/position)

Paul still can't *get over* Doris completely. (= become emotionally indifferent)

At meetings, the others never let me *get* my views *across.* (= communicate; make . . . understand)

Stop talking about the weather and *get down to* business. (= start discussing the main topic)

I'll never *get through* all these Christmas cards in one day. (= be able to complete . . .)

How can your parents and teachers *get through to* you? (= make . . . understand; "connect" with someone— literally and figuratively)

We usually *get the mail* around 11:00. (= receive letters/packages)

This firm's employees *get paid* monthly. (= receive salary)

It usually takes 15 minutes *to get to* the mall from here. (= reach/arrive at a place)

I just *got home* from work. (= returned to my house from the office)

We *got back* from the beach a few minutes ago. (= returned from a place)

d. Positive and negative prefixes

Many words in English add extra meanings or nuances through the use of prefixes and suffixes. They not only allow us to increase vocabulary, but also add certain positive or negative qualities to existing nouns and adjectives—as well as to a few verbs and adverbs. There are many suffixes and prefixes, and each one adds its own shading to the existing word's meaning. Certain prefixes and suffixes can actually change the meaning of a word—particularly nouns—or sometimes even change the word itself. There are probably hundreds of prefixes and suffixes; here we give only a few to help you understand their effect on English vocabulary. If a prefix or suffix is used with nouns, adjectives, and possibly other grammar forms, each will be indicated.

Here are some positive prefixes:

- *hyper-* means "very" or "excessively"

hyperactive (adj.)	→→→	**That boy never sits still. He's *hyperactive*!**
hypercritical (adj.)	→→→	**Nothing pleases Scott lately; he's become *hypercritical*.**
hypersensitive (adj.)	→→→	**Tara's skin is so *hypersensitive*, she can't use any makeup.**

- *multi-* means "many"

multifaceted (adj.)	→→→	**Aaron has so many talents—he's really a *multifaceted* person.**
multifunctional (adj.)	→→→	**This piece of furniture is *multifunctional*—it can be used in many ways.**
multisided (adj.)	→→→	**This is a *multisided* issue.**
multivitamin (n.)	→→→	**To be sure of getting all necessary nutrients, my doctor recommended a *multivitamin*.**

- *ultra-* means "beyond average" or "extremely"

ultramodern	→→→	**Their new house is so *ultramodern*, it's spaceage!**

THE COMPLEX SENTENCE

ultraconservative	→→→	I wouldn't wear that tie—bankers are expected to be *ultraconservative*, you know.
ultraviolent	→→→	I'll never let my kids watch this kind of *ultraviolent* movie.
ultraquiet	→→→	We love our new *ultraquiet* air conditioner.
ultrachic	→→→	That silver watch of Helen's was *ultrachic* last year, but it's become too popular now.

Here are some negative prefixes:

- *dis-* can mean "not," but it can also mean "opposite" or "apart" *

disadvantage (n.)	→→→	Helen is at a professional *disadvantage* by not having an advanced degree in her field.
disinterested (adj.)**	→→→	Joe is a completely *disinterested* person in this area.
disuse (n.)	→→→	The habit of using calling cards in private life has fallen into *disuse*.
disinclined (adj.)	→→→	I'm *disinclined* to interfere in my children's married lives.

Note: *Be careful of the spelling. The negative prefix *dys-* means "impaired" or "bad."

Note: **The *dis-* of *disinterested* means "apart." A *disinterested* person is objective, uninvolved; an *uninterested* person has no interest, is bored, etc.

- *un-* means "not," and is usually the most clearly negative prefix

unable (adj.)	→→→	**He's either *unable* or *unwilling* to change his behavior.**
unskilled (adj.)	→→→	**The available labor pool is mostly *unskilled*.**
unaware (adj.)	→→→	**I was completely *unaware* of Hannah's problems.**

- *mis-* means "incorrectly," "badly," or "poorly done"; it doesn't just mean "not"

misplaced (v.) & (adj.)	→→→	**Mrs. Winslow's confidence in her lawyer was totally *misplaced*.**
misguided (adj.)	→→→	**The school was very *misguided* in its attempts to change Brian.**
mishandle (v.)	→→→	**You've thoroughly *mishandled* this situation by *misusing* your authority.**
misinformed (adj.)	→→→	**You've been *misinformed*, and that newspaper story was also full of *misinformation*.**

- *non-* also means "not," but it's really closer to "missing" or "doesn't exist"

nonexistent (adj.)	→→→	**Harry's savings are *nonexistent*.**
nonfunctional (adj.)	→→→	**This sink is just for decoration— it's completely *nonfunctional*.**
nonconformist (n.)	→→→	**The 1960s produced more *nonconformists* than the 1980s did.**
nonsmoker (n.)	→→→	**Everyone in this office is a *nonsmoker*.**

THE COMPLEX SENTENCE

e. Positive and negative suffixes

Unlike the prefixes, these suffixes are each largely able to be both positive and negative, depending on the adjective they are used with.

- *-able* (also *-ible*) means "capable of," "can," "is needed"

acceptable	→→→	This is *acceptable* quality.
recognizable	→→→	Movie stars' faces were very *recognizable* once, now they seem *interchangeable*.
suitable	→→→	My parents said Tom was *unsuitable* as a possible husband so that made him completely *suitable* in my eyes.
preferable	→→→	Tea is *preferable* to coffee, but all caffeine is bad for me.

- *-ous* means "like" or "connected with"

courageous	→→→	Daddy's been so *courageous* throughout this ordeal.
dangerous	→→→	Chris isn't merely reckless—he's a truly *dangerous* driver.
studious	→→→	Sam is both *studious* and ambitious.

- *-ful* means "full of"

useful	→→→	This kind of can opener is really *useful*, but the last one you bought was completely *useless*.
successful	→→→	Your father made some very *successful* stock speculations.
hopeful	→→→	I'm *hopeful* for the future.

distrustful	→→→	**Wallace was very trusting as a boy, but he has become very *distrustful* as an adult.**

- *-less* means "lacking" or "without," but can be used to mean lacking in bad as well as good qualities; often the opposite of many adjectives ending with the suffix *-ful*

selfless	→→→	**She's a wonderfully *selfless* wife and mother.**
harmless	→→→	**Don't worry, this soap is completely *harmless* to pets.**
thoughtless	→→→	**Harry is such a *thoughtless* child, and his brother Jack is so *thoughtful*.**
careless	→→→	**Why are you so *careless* with your clothes?**
joyless	→→→	**The professor is such a *joyless* person.**

APPENDIXES

Ⓐ Punctuation, Spelling, Capital Letters

Punctuation

Punctuation is a very complicated subject because there are many shadings of language that can be changed by the addition, substitution, or change in a single mark of punctuation. Following are only the most basic rules.

Periods

We use periods:

- to show where a statement, either affirmative or negative, ends

Please call a doctor.
My number is 235-2774.
This my daughter.

- after an abbreviation

Mr.	**Ave.**
Inc.	**U.S.**

- after individual item numbers in a vertical list

1. group sales
2. individual sales
3. customer service

Commas

We use commas:

- to separate three or more items in a horizontal list*

coffee, tea, or milk
strawberries, raspberries, blueberries, melons, and peaches

Note: *The comma always comes before *and, but, or,* etc.

- to separate the two parts of a long sentence if the parts are really two short sentences

Betty wanted to see a movie, but Anne was hungry and insisted on lunch.

- to separate two clauses

This model, which is probably our biggest seller, costs $2,800.
After Dad was hospitalized, we had to cancel the trip.
If the rain stops, we'll play ball.

- to separate the question tag from the statement part of tag questions

He's always late, isn't he?
You live near the harbor, don't you?

227

• to separate the numbers in four- or more digit figures

1,000
$180,000
20,000 people
5,000,000 units

Question marks

We use question marks:

• at the end of simple questions

Who is it?
What time are we going?

• at the end of tag questions, negative questions, and rhetorical questions

It's too hot, isn't it?
Don't drivers use their turn signals anymore?
Who thought up this procedure?

Exclamation points

We use exclamation points:

• to show enthusiasm

That's great!
Wonderful meal!

- to give "commands" using imperative verb forms

Stop that right now!
Don't touch that!

- to show surprise (sometimes replaces a question mark)

Henry! I never thought we'd meet again.
You're married!

Spelling

There are many spelling changes in English. Following are some basic guidelines. Remember that vowels are the letters *a, e, i, o,* and *u*; consonants are all other letters.

- Words ending in a single consonant following a *single* vowel double the last consonant before the tense endings *-ed* and *-ing:*

begin →→→ begin**n**ing
swim →→→ swim**m**ing
set →→→ set**t**ing
dig →→→ dig**g**ing
forbid →→→ forbid**d**ing
sin →→→ sin**n**ed
fit →→→ fit**t**ed

- All words ending in *-e*, drop the *-e* before the tense endings *-ed* and *-ing:*

bak**e** →→→ bak**ing**
bak**e** →→→ bak**ed**
lov**e** →→→ lov**ing**
love →→→ lov**ed**

Exception: verbs ending in *-ee* keep the second *-e.*

agr<u>ee</u> →→→ agr<u>ee</u>***d***
agr<u>ee</u> →→→ agr<u>ee</u>***ing***
s<u>ee</u> →→→ s<u>ee</u>***ing***

- For the third person (*he, she, it*) verb ending in the simple present *and* the plural form of any noun ending in *-sh, -ch, -ss, -x,* and *-o, -s* becomes *-es.*

d<u>o</u> →→→ d<u>o</u>***es***
g<u>o</u> →→→ g<u>o</u>***es***
pu<u>sh</u> →→→ pu<u>sh</u>***es***
tou<u>ch</u> →→→ tou<u>ch</u>***es***
bo<u>ss</u> →→→ bo<u>ss</u>***es***
bo<u>x</u> →→→ bo<u>x</u>***es***

- For *most* adjectives that become *-ly* adverbs, the following changes are made:

  adjectives ending in *-ic* usually change to *-ally*

automat<u>ic</u> →→→ automat<u>ic</u>**ally**
fantast<u>ic</u> →→→ fantast<u>ic</u>**ally**
systemat<u>ic</u> →→→ systemat<u>ic</u>**ally**

  adjectives ending in *-l* usually keep the final *-l,* making the adverb form's ending *-lly*

cynica<u>l</u> →→→ cynica**lly**
gratefu<u>l</u> →→→ gratefu**lly**
fearfu<u>l</u> →→→ fearfu**lly**

adjectives ending in *-le* change the *-le* to *-ly* in the adverb form

regrettab<u>le</u> →→→ regrettab**ly**

humb<u>le</u> →→→ humb**ly**

terrib<u>le</u> →→→ terrib**ly**

adjectives ending in *-y* change the final *-y* to *-ily* after the final consonant

hast<u>y</u> →→→ hast**ily**

eas<u>y</u> →→→ eas**ily**

bus<u>y</u> →→→ bus**ily**

- For the <u>past</u> tense of verbs that end in *-y,* and for the plurals of nouns ending in *-y*: if the *-y* comes after a single or double consonant, it changes to *-ied* or *-ies,* respectively, but if it comes after a vowel, the *-y* doesn't change.

cr<u>y</u> →→→ cr**ied**

carr<u>y</u> →→→ carr**ied**

tr<u>y</u> →→→ tr**ied**

worr<u>y</u> →→→ worr**ied**

lad<u>y</u> →→→ lad**ies**

BUT

stra<u>y</u> →→→ stra**yed**

to<u>y</u> →→→ to**ys**

- Verbs that end in *-ie* change to *-y* before an *-ing* form.

l<u>ie</u> →→→ l**y**ing

d<u>ie</u> →→→ d**y**ing

APPENDIXES

Capital letters

English uses capital letters for these things:

- the first letter of any sentence

Dinner is ready.
Are you hungry?

- people's first and last names, and any middle initials

Joe
Paula Emerson
Mary-Sue McVey
Gerald B. Croft

- names of pets or some breeds of animal

my poodle, Folly
the famous racehorse, Midnight
Persian cats
an Afghan hound
Skye terriers
Bengal tigers

- the pronoun *I*

Wherever I go, I take along a bottle of water.

- common nouns that are used as titles when we are talking directly to the person, or using that person's name and title together

Hi, Mom. →→→ **My mom makes great cookies.**

I saw Uncle Bob at the market. →→→ **You know my uncle, Bob Patterson, don't you?**

Tell me, Doctor, is this medicine safe? →→→ **My doctor is very cautious.**

I learned in school that President Lincoln was shot at the theater. →→→ **The president of the PTA has five daughters.**

Also, the titles *Mr., Ms., Mrs.,* and *Miss* are always written with the first letter capitalized.

- common nouns or adjectives resulting from a person's name

That marketing strategy of yours was truly Machiavellian.

They live in a Victorian cottage.

The building is in the early Federal style of the 1820s.

- the names of holidays, days of the week, and months*

In the United States, national elections are held on the second Tuesday in November.

The official beginning of summer is June 21st.

What day does Christmas fall on this year?

Margaret's birthday is next Saturday, February 8th.

Note: *The names of seasons are rarely capitalized in modern English.

- the names of countries, languages, and nationalities; almost all adjectives for countries

Gérard is French; he comes from the Loire Valley.

She speaks both Castillian Spanish and the Basque language.

Conjugating adjectives is a feature of Germanic languages.

I can't read this—it's written in the Cyrillic alphabet.

- cities, provinces, regions, states, and all adjectives related to them

Janet stayed in Boston after graduating from Harvard.

This is a Napa Valley wine.

Look at all this beautiful Venetian glass.

Most hurricanes affect the Gulf states. (= U.S. states bordering the Gulf of Mexico)

My mother's wedding dress was made of Lyonnaise velvet.

- the names of compass locations *if* they represent a region (*not* for directions)

This soup is a specialty of the Pacific Northwest. (BUT *We're first going to fly northwest, then due north*)

Chiang Mai is the largest city in the North, and the second largest in Thailand.

How would American history have changed if the South had won the Civil War?

- the names of oceans, lakes, rivers, etc.

the Pacific Ocean	**Niagara Falls**
the Rhine River	**Lake Geneva**
the Hudson River	**the Caspian Sea**

- the names of eras or events in history

the Norman Conquest
the French Revolution
the Reformation
the T'ang Dynasty

- street and business names

Park Avenue
the corner of Madison Avenue and East 52nd Street
Oxford Street
Microsoft Systems, Inc.
Berlitz Publishing Company, Inc.

- the names of parks, gardens, and many buildings (office buildings, theaters, public buildings, etc.)

Hyde Park
the Bronx Botanical Gardens
the World Trade Center

- book, film, play, opera, newspaper, magazine, and song titles**

> *Catcher in the Rye*
> *Gone with the Wind*
> *Long Day's Journey into Night*
> *Wall Street Journal*
> *Harper's Bazaar*
> *As Time Goes By***

Note: **In all titles, these things are generally *not* capitalized: articles (*a, an, the*); short prepositions (*in, at, by, on, of, out, as, to,* etc.); conjunctions (*and, but, or, nor,* and *if*); and the *to* of a verb's infinitive form (*to be*). Exceptions: longer prepositions such as *among, between, about,* etc.; anything that starts or ends a sentence; the article *the* is capitalized only if it is part of the name of a creative work or publication (*The New York Times* →→→ *the Sacramento Bee*).

- paintings, sculptures, etc.

> *The Blue Boy,* by Gainsborough
> Rembrandt's *The Night Watch*
> *The Thinker,* by Rodin

Irregular Verbs

Present	Past	Past Participle
A		
arise	arose	arisen
awake	awoke	awoken
B		
be	was/were	been
bear	bore	born
beat	beat	beaten
become	became	become
begin	began	begun
behold	beheld	beheld
bend	bent	bent
bet	bet	bet
bid	bid	bid
bind	bound	bound
bite	bit	bitten
bleed	bled	bled
blow	blew	blown
break	broke	broken
breed	bred	bred
bring	brought	brought
broadcast	broadcast	broadcast
build	built	built
burn	burned	burned
burst	burst	burst
buy	bought	bought
C		
catch	caught	caught
choose	chose	chosen
cling	clung	clung
come	came	come
cost	cost	cost
creep	crept	crept
cut	cut	cut

APPENDIXES

Present	Past	Past Participle
D		
deal	dealt	dealt
dig	dug	dug
do	did	done
draw	drew	drawn
dream	dreamed	dreamed
drink	drank	drunk
drive	drove	driven
E		
eat	ate	eaten
F		
fall	fell	fallen
feed	fed	fed
feel	felt	felt
fight	fought	fought
find	found	found
fit	fit	fit
flee	fled	fled
fling	flung	flung
fly	flew	flown
forbid	forbade	forbidden
forecast	forecast	forecast
foresee	foresaw	foreseen
forget	forgot	forgotten
forgive	forgave	forgiven
forsake	forsook	forsaken
freeze	froze	frozen
G		
get	got	gotten/got
give	gave	given
go	went	gone
grow	grew	grown
H		
hang	hung	hung
have	had	had
hear	heard	heard
hide	hid	hidden
hit	hit	hit
hold	held	held
hurt	hurt	hurt

Present	Past	Past Participle
I		
input	input	input
K		
keep	kept	kept
kneel	knelt/kneeled	knelt/kneeled
knit	knit/knitted	knit/knitted
know	knew	known
L		
lay	laid	laid
lead	led	led
lean	leaned	leaned
leap	leapt/leaped	leapt/leaped
learn	learned	learned
leave	left	left
lend	lent	lent
let	let	let
lie	lay	lain
light	lit	lit
lose	lost	lost
M		
make	made	made
mean	meant	meant
meet	met	met
mishear	misheard	misheard
mislay	mislaid	mislaid
mislead	misled	misled
misread	misread	misread
misspell	misspelled/misspelt	misspelled/misspelt
mistake	mistook	mistaken
misunderstand	misunderstood	misunderstood
mow	mowed	mowed
O		
outbid	outbid	outbid
outdo	outdid	outdone
outgrow	outgrew	outgrown
outrun	outran	outrun
outsell	outsold	outsold
overcast	overcast	overcast
overcome	overcame	overcome

Present	Past	Past Participle

O

Present	Past	Past Participle
overdo	overdid	overdone
overdraw	overdrew	overdrawn
overeat	overate	overeaten
overhang	overhung	overhung
overhear	overheard	overheard
overpay	overpaid	overpaid
override	overrode	overridden
overrun	overran	overrun
oversee	oversaw	overseen
oversell	oversold	oversold
oversleep	overslept	overslept
overtake	overtook	overtaken
overthrow	overthrew	overthrown

P

Present	Past	Past Participle
pay	paid	paid
plead	pled/pleaded	pled/pleaded
pre-set	pre-set	pre-set
proofread	proofread	proofread
prove	proved	proven/proved
put	put	put

Q

Present	Past	Past Participle
quit	quit/quitted	quit/quitted

R

Present	Past	Past Participle
read	read	read
rebind	rebound	rebound
rebuild	rebuilt	rebuilt
redo	redid	redone
remake	remade	remade
repay	repaid	repaid
rerun	reran	rerun
resell	resold	resold
reset	reset	reset
rethink	rethought	rethought
rewind	rewound	rewound
rewrite	rewrote	rewritten
rid	rid	rid
ride	rode	ridden
ring	rang	rung
rise	rose	risen
run	ran	run

Present	Past	Past Participle

S

Present	Past	Past Participle
say	said	said
see	saw	seen
seek	sought	sought
sell	sold	sold
send	sent	sent
set	set	set
sew	sewed	sewn/sewed
shake	shook	shaken
shed	shed	shed
shine	shined/shone	shined/shone
shoot	shot	shot
show	showed	shown
shrink	shrank/shrunk	shrunk
shut	shut	shut
sing	sang	sung
sit	sat	sat
sleep	slept	slept
slide	slid	slid
smell	smelled	smelled
speak	spoke	spoken
speed	sped	sped
spell	spelled	spelled
spend	spent	spent
spin	spun	spun
split	split	split
spoil	spoiled	spoiled
spread	spread	spread
spring	sprang/sprung	sprung
stand	stood	stood
steal	stole	stolen
stick	stuck	stuck
sting	stung	stung
strike (hit)	struck	struck/stricken
string	strung	strung
strive	strove	striven
swear	swore	sworn
sweep	swept	swept
swell	swelled	swollen
swim	swam	swum
swing	swung	swung

Present	Past	Past Participle
T		
take	took	taken
teach	taught	taught
tear	tore	torn
tell	told	told
think	thought	thought
throw	threw	thrown
U		
underlie	underlay	underlain
understand	understood	understood
undertake	undertook	undertaken
underwrite	underwrote	underwritten
undo	undid	undone
unwind	unwound	unwound
uphold	upheld	upheld
upset	upset	upset
W		
wake	woke	woken
wear	wore	worn
wed	wed	wed
weep	wept	wept
wet	wet	wet
win	won	won
wind	wound	wound
withdraw	withdrew	withdrawn
write	wrote	written

INDEX

INDEX

INDEX

INDEX